Abandon Hope, All
Ye Who Enter Here

Cad
A Handbook For Heels

Feral House

CAD is dedicated:

"... to the moral ones upon whom Beauty exercises a lascivious and corrupting influence; to the moral ones who have relentlessly chased God out of their bedrooms; to the moral ones who cringe before Nature, who flatten themselves upon prayer rugs, who shut their eyes, stuff their ears, bind, gag and truss themselves and offer their mutilations to the idiot God they have invented, to the anointed ones who have slain themselves and who stagger proudly into graves; to the religious ones who wage bloody and tireless wars upon all who do not share their fear of life; to the prim ones who find their secret obscenities mirrored in every careless phrase; to the cowardly ones who borrow their courage from Ideals which they forthwith defend with their useless lives; to the cowardly ones who adorn themselves with castrations; to the reformers — the psychopathic ones trying forever to drown their own obscene desires in ear-splitting prayers for their fellowman's welfare; to the reformers — the Freudian dervishes who masturbate with Purity Leagues, who achieve involved orgasms denouncing the depravities of others; to the reformers, the psychopathic ones who seek to vindicate their own sexual impotencies by padlocking the national vagina; to the ostracizing ones who hurl excommunication upon all that is not part of their stupidity; to the pious ones who, lacking the strength to please themselves, boast interminably to God of their weakness in denying themselves; to the smug ones who walk with their noses ecstatically buried in their own rectums; to the righteous ones who masturbate blissfully under the blankets of their perfections; to the conservative ones who gnaw elatedly upon old bones and wither with malnutrition; to the timorous ones who vomit invective upon all that confuses them, who vituperate against all their non-existent intelligence cannot grasp; to the intellectual ones who play solitaire with platitudes, who drag their classrooms around with them; to these and to many other abominations who I apologize to for omitting, this book is dedicated in the hope that their righteous eyes may never kindle with secret lusts nor their pious lips water erotically from its reading ..."

— Ben Hecht, *Fantazius Mallare*

Schneider

Parfrey

Cooper

Lindgren

Krafft

Clowes

Roderick

Chic

Peeping

Blackburn

Man, it's dismal out there! You want to read a magazine, and it's either a textbook lesson in gynecology or some celebrity sheet slanted to the purple set. You hear about a men's movement, and it turns out to be a lot of touchy-feely poet stuff in the woods (maybe they'd be better off frequenting the johns on the interstate). You think, what the hell is going on? What's a red-blooded American male to do? Friends, look no further. CAD'll make you want stand up and salute, what with our carload of talent of the two-fisted *and* two-breasted variety.

Maybe you've heard about that South Sea rogue, **Edgar Leeteg,** grandaddy of black velvet art. **Charles Krafft** takes us to the Tahitian hideout of this inveterate womanizer, boozer, mother-lover and cadish artistic innovator. Another of our favorite artists, jazz stylist **Chet Baker,** provides a terrifying confession of heroin addiction and confinement to the hoosegows and hell-holes of Europe.

Russ Meyer, the man who singlehandedly defined the male obsession for female breastworks in the late twentieth century, is interviewed by **Sergei Hasenecz** and editor **Charles Schneider** on all manner of topics relevant to cads. (By the way, it's Meyer's photograph of his luscious first wife, **Eve,** that graces the cover.) Meyer made his start with burlesque entrepreneur Pete De Cenzie, and so it's only fitting that CAD toasts this much-missed form of male entertainment in informative articles by **Walt Fishman, Doug Bonde** and **Milton Machlin.**

If you wanted to know about whips and women but didn't know who to ask, our own **Roderick Thorndyke** at last gives you the low-down. If you haven't been man enough to light up a big, fragrant cigar in public, **Brian Chic's** "Havana Smoke" might inspire you to do so. And if something has really been amiss in the testosterone department, read my short history on such mad scientist rejuvenation cures such as Serge Voronoff's monkey testicle transplant operation.

Connoisseurs of the female form will find their meat, drink and smoke in our prurient profiles of **Lilly Christine, Tina Louise, June Wilkinson, Debra Lamb** and **Laura Richmond,** the latter pair masterfully photographed by CAD's own **Scott Lindgren.**

Our how-to departments are skillfully manned (and womaned) by gastronomic and Orphic experts as **Kyle Roderick, Dick Blackburn** and **Jerry Nutter.**

It takes a special kind of talent to tell an old story in a new way. **Daniel Clowes'** "Frankie and Johnny" and **Tom Peeping's** "HMS Terrible" takes familiar chestnuts and roasts them on a new, daft fire. And if that ain't enough, ogle the amazing pen-work of CAD artiste **Chris Cooper,** better known to the world as the ubiquitous "Coop," and **Cliff Mott's** totally cracked 'toon on how men might better put to use that appliance popularly known as the brassiere.

Read it and weep — weep that you haven't seen CAD on the stands until now!

Adam Parfrey, Feral House

CAD, my honored wolves, is a unique publication, a treasure-trove of information, both useful and otherwise. There is something for every man inside. Something to turn the most lily-livered sap into a rapacious rogue.

The stories are of the two-fisted kind, ones that keep you virile, alert and on the prowl.

And the gag cartoons! You'll bust your BVD's over this collection of salty side-splitters.

And lest we forget, in these pages you will find, you lucky, snarling rascals, the most exotic, charming, bewitching, glamorous and glorious girls shown the way nature intended 'em!

So take 'em to your lair, we've done our part.

Put your feet up, light up a fragrant stogie, have the lady mix you a martini, relax, and enjoy.

— Charles Schneider, Editor

CONTENTS

Departments

Humor

Pictorials

Fiction

Articles

PUBLISHER
Adam Parfrey

EDITOR
Charles Schneider

ART DIRECTOR
Linda Hayashi

ART PRODUCTION
Chris Cooper

Cadwallader
J. Cadd

In some civilizations, it is perfectly correct and proper for a man without embarrassment or penalty to accost a girl who catches his eye. Unfortunly, we live in a culture that frowns on such behavior.

A well-behaved man of our civilization may not approach a girl who appeals to him unless formally introduced. Any attempt to by-pass this pattern stamps him as a cad, a low-born bounder or a fresh thing.

However, cads — low-born bounders and "fresh things" — enjoy a delightful standard of living. Should you wish to emulate them, there are certain things you should know. It is not as easy to be a cad as it might seem.

The science of cadism depends on the ability to reverse ordinary behavior. You must forget everything you've been taught. You must say to yourself, over and over, "I'm a cad and, hence, not bound by normal rules of conduct."

And then you must suit your actions to your words.

Picture this scene. You are at a literary tea. It is being given in honor of say, a woman named Iphogenia Tarte, a tribute to her latest volume of verse. "In Praise of Chipmunks." As always, you are correct and proper, sipping your tea like a little gentleman and ignoring the fact that Miss Tarte has a shape like a stone outbuilding and is winking at you between each couplet.

A gentleman would ignore the hussy. Not so a cad.

He would smile at her gently and, in an opportune moment, seize destiny in both hands and approach her directly.

"Miss Tarte," he will say, pouring her some tea, "what say we stop drinking this slop and get our stomachs around something with a little more class. Up at my place, I've got a fresh bottle of gin, a few etchings to lend the joint some tone, and a newly-made double bed."

"Call me Iphogenia." she'll say, as you walk out hand in hand. As the two of you leave, chances are good that you will pass a few gentlemen, still sipping tea and discussing the last sonnet. They've obeyed the code; they are the happy ones. But you, you cad, you've got Iphogenia and misery.

Is that what you want? If it is, go to it. Remember, however, that you are making your own bed. Once a cad, always a cad. There's no turning back. Put your cherished moral code behind you. Ahead lies unhappiness, a disturbed conscience and lots of beautiful girls.

You will find, as your career as a cad continues, that Iphogenia Tarte is the exception. She is an emancipated woman; as free in her way as you are in yours. Very few girls have the moral liberty to be that forward. Generally, you will find, girls are bound by some moral code that once imprisoned you. It is a ridiculous code, but there it is.

Usually, you will have to make the first advance. In some circles, this is known as making "a pass." It is a fine art, on an equal plane with painting a portrait, writing a play or mugging an old lady.

Rules of conduct for making passes cannot be set down exactly. The situation determines the technique. In some situations, a simple wave of a bill will be sufficient to break the ice. In others, a much more complicated strategy must of necessity be employed. You must size up the situation as though you were a general commanding an army, looking over the terrain, probing for weak spots, estimating your own strength and advantages.

What are the inherent advantages of a cad? He is, first and foremost, a male. With the ordinary female, that immediately gives him a head start. But, in itself, it is not enough. A cad is ordinarily possessed of a certain brashness and boldness of attitude that generally appeals to an impressionable female. She is used to gentlemen; the opposite, because of its unique appearance, will often prove attractive.

So the first thing a budding cad should realize is that he must emphasize his masculinity and his fresh approach. A beard is helpful in achieving the former aim. And a cocky smile is a sure way of tipping off the latter.

Fine. We find you at this tea party, wearing a beard and a cocky smile. Across the way are three girls. Since they also wear beards and cocky smiles, it is best to ignore them. They are probably imposters.

But, over there by the Duncan Phyfe highboy, what is that? It is a sexy blond, or else a reasonably accurate facsimile. Let her be the target for tonight, the object of our scientific research into true cad behavior.

First, we aim our beard and cocky smile in her direction. She turns back. Good! It is a charming back. And it is good to have some small degree of resistance. It makes the game that much more challenging and entertaining.

We approach, sizing up every factor we know as we walk across the rooom. What do we know? She is female hence flattery is a potent weapon. She is blonde and beautiful, so she is most likely experienced. Hence flattery isn't so potent a weapon. She is exceedingly well dressed, hence probably wealthy. A gift would probably not impress her. But she is female, so a gift might be the very thing.

As we near the spot where she stands, we sum up what we know.

We know nothing.

So we start from scratch.

"I beg your pardon," she says. "I am not itchy, so why do you scratch my back?"

"I am starting in from scratch," you say, wagging your beard roguishly.

"Very funny," she says, emptying a pot of scalding hot tea down your front.

"I take my tea with lemon," you

GRADE-A CAD

say, trying to make best of a bad situation.

"If that's the way you want it, OK," she says, squirting you full in the face with a juicy one.

"Ah, that's better," you say, still outwardly brave.

"Do you take cream?" she asks, innocently.

"No, thanks," you say. Enough's enough.

"That's too bad." And she turns on her heel and walks away briskly, with the air of a hunter who has just downed a fine three-pointer.

You dry yourself off and return to the fray. It's like they advise people who've had auto accidents — get right back in the car and drive. And so you, too, should follow each rebuff with an immediate resumption of hostilities. In the long run, that's the best way to keep up your all-important nerve.

So you spot the blond again, over by a Heeplewhite lowboy. And you give her the old waggling beard and cocky smile.

"Say, there," you say, "haven't we met before?"

"Yes, I think so," she says. "Care for some more tea?"

"No, not just now. Thanks awfully. I was going to suggest we skip out of here and..."

"Drop suddenly and completely dead."

And she turns on her heel — the other one, this time — and walks away. You are left with egg on your face. It goes well with your beard.

Your mind is made up. You are determined. Dark flashes of courage light your eyes. You look around the room. She is standing by a Chippendale mediumboy. You approach.

"Look miss," you begin.

"Oh, hello, there, " she says with a warm smile. "I'd like you to meet my friend Charlie Chippendale. My name is Mona Lowe. And you are — ?"

You introduce yourself. She smiles, shakes hands in a hearty manner. You smile, give Chippendale the "get-lost-pal" look and he gets lost.

"How about a spin in my Jaguar?"

"Love to."

"And then up to my place for a nightcap?"

"Divine."

"And then, afterwards, who can tell?"

"Who, indeed!"

What accounts for this sudden change, this amazing reversal in form? She attacked you with tea and lemon the first time, told you to drop dead the second time and then, on the third approach, succumbed easily to your many charms. How come?

The answer, you will find is the keystone of cadism. It is persistence. You cannot expect a nice girl to fall all over you the first time. She has her pride, her vestiges of moral scruples. She must put on an act. The third time (maybe it won't be until the fourth or fifth) she will be ready. While you were sizing her up, she was sizing you up. Two play at the game. You must allow her time to keep her pride, estimate your appeal and cancel previous engagements.

Plot. Persistence. Confidence.

You cannot fail. You will be a real louse.

— *Winston Peabody*

13

Cads and Dolls

CHARM IS A WAY OF
GETTING THE ANSWER
YES WITHOUT ASKING
A CLEAR QUESTION.
ALBERT CAMUS

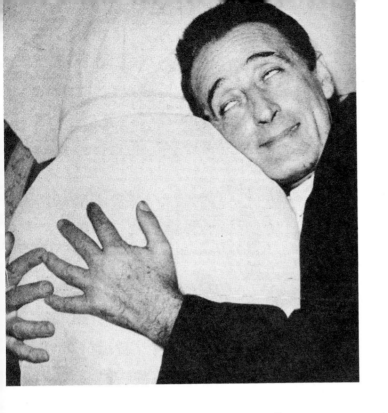

BELLADONNA, n. in italian, a beautiful lady: in english, a deadly poison. a striking example of the essential identity of the two tongues.

AMBROSE BIERCE

LICENSE MY ROVING HANDS, AND LET THEM GO, BEFORE, BEHIND, BETWEEN, ABOVE, BELOW.

JOHN DONNE

Cads and Dolls

cads and dolls

THE ETERNAL FEMALE DRAWS US ONWARD.
GOETHE

PEOPLE WILL
INSIST . . .
ON TREATING
THE MONS VENERIS
AS THOUGH IT WERE
MOUNT EVEREST.
ALDOUS HUXLEY

CADS
AND
DOLLS

CAD's Culinary

Like most modern guys, you're probably a greenhorn when it comes to cooking techniques, but you'd still prefer blissful ignorance to reading one of those fancy la-de-da cookbooks that housewives swoon over.

You're famous in your set for popping bright questions like, "Which one's the stove?" On those rare occasions when you're home and need to put on the old feedbag, sardines straight from the can — piled on toast — is your idea of a swell meal. What's more, you feel compelled to learn how to operate a blender.

Think of this as more than just a bunch of menus for knuckleheads who can't boil water. Face it, you need to learn how to cook ASAP so you can invite dames to your pad under legitimate pretenses.

(Note: Don't be fooled. These recipes work.)

DISHES FOR THE MORNING AFTER

SAMOAN LOVE KABOBS

This aphrodisiac hors d'oeuvre really hits the spot at a cocktail party or as an appetizer for a tete-a-tete dinner. Here's how you whip it up:

Cut up small cubes of pork tenderloin and ready-to-eat ham (enough for you and your guests). Place ham cubes in one bowl, pork in another. Splash enough red wine over the pork to make a good marinade, let sit for a half hour. On skewers, alternate canned pineapple chunks with the ham and pork cubes. Grill under the broiler — or the barbecue — just long enough to brown lightly.

LA DOLCE VELVEETA MUFFINS

Here's a nice 'n' easy canape (it's pronounced can-a-pay, for you fellows who slept through conversational French) that's an All-American treat. You'll need a blender to prepare this, so hie yourself down to the hardware store and buy one! Incidentally, this dish works well for cocktails, dinner, midnight snacks, or even better — for breakfast after a dreamy night.

1 pound Velveeta cheese, grated

2 cups milk

2 rounded tablespoons of flour

1/4 tsp. mustard

1/4 tsp. brown sugar

2 shallot or green onion, minced

1 tsp. MSG (monosodium glutamate — it's a powder that brings out the flavor in foods)

1/4 tsp. Worcestershire sauce

1 package of English muffins

Fresh ground pepper and a dash of salt

Ready-to-serve Canadian bacon for garnishing

Pour milk in electric blender, add flour, and whizz. Add all dry ingredients, onion, and Worcestershire sauce. Pour this mixture into a medium size saucepan and heat, stirring constantly until hot, then add grated cheese. When it is melted, taste and add more salt and pepper if desired. Pour over toasted English muffins, scatter some fine chunks of Velveeta on top and pop into the oven at 375 degrees until the cheese has melted just a tad. Place ready-to-serve Canadian bacon, finely sliced, atop each muffin. Bake until bacon starts to curl: now they're ready to be enjoyed.

PATÉ DE SPAM

Move over, paté de foie gras, and make room for this moderne delicacy. At about one-tenth of the price of goose liver paté, paté de Spam sends most discerning noshers over the moon with mouth-watering satisfaction. This robust paté keeps a week or so in the fridge, and can be served any hour of the day or night on toast, crackers, or crusty French bread.

1 can Spam (12 oz.)

8 ounces liver sausage

1 hard boiled egg

1 tsp. Gulden's hot mustard

Dash each of pepper, nutmeg, cinnamon, Tabasco sauce

1 oz. Calvados brandy

1 tsp. soft butter

2 black truffles, diced

Dig out a half can of Spam and place it as well as the other ingredients (except truffles) into a top speed blender. Blend until smooth. Put mixture into a glass or metal dish; sprinkle truffles on top and chill in fridge overnight so ingredients can "marry". Serve the paté on fine china with sprigs of parsley and cherry tomatoes surrounding meat. Melba toast, Ritz crackers, French bread are suitable for spreading this paté.

Companion

BY KYLE RODERICK

WILDLIFE

TWO-FISTED PHEASANT

Everyone enjoys a shot of Jack Daniels after a hard day, and just about every homo erectus worth his salt needs to tuck into some game birds at least once a hunting season. Here's a knock-out meal that combines two first-rate delicacies — Jack Daniels and pheasant.

Method:

Start with 2 properly aged pheasant. Remove the breasts and legs and dredge them in flour. Saute them in butter over gentle flame. Place the pheasant in a Dutch oven or heavy pot with a lid and add 2 large shallots, finely chopped, and 1/2 pound of fresh mushrooms which have been sauteed first in butter. Pour two ounces — hell, three, if you're feeling festive — over this mixture, and season with salt and pepper. Make a stock with the backs or use chicken broth and add enough of this broth from time to time so the pheasant doesn't burn but will make a thick sauce. Let the birds simmer lightly for about an hour, or until tender. Add a teaspoon of MSG (monosodium glutamate) and about ten minutes before serving whip a 1/2 pint of sour cream and stir it into the pheasant. Let the cream heat through and serve with wild rice on the side plus a green salad.

BRAISED IGUANA WITH VEGETABLES

If you're ever in the Southwest and you find yourself a few bucks short of a meal, you can always try catching an iguana, a.k.a. giant lizard. Iguana meat tastes rather like chicken, and in some parts of the desert, it's a staple.

Cleaning the Iguana:

Draw the animal in half; skin the legs and cut off the head and tail. Roast the meat in the skin after washing it thoroughly in several cold waters. Soak overnight in slightly salted cold water.

Braising the Iguana with Vegetables:

Take the required amount of iguana meat, which has been prepared according to the above guidelines. Place it in rapidly boiling salt water and parboil it for thirty minutes. Remove from water; drain, wipe dry, roll in flour and fry brown in hot pork lard — or Crisco if you can't find pork lard. When browned, take from the pan and set aside in a warm place until ready to use. Now drain off all but 2 tablespoons of the oil in which the meat was cooked. Place the pan back on the heat over a low flame and add the following:

1 or 2 onions, sliced

2 carrots, diced

2 potatoes, cubed

3 tomatoes, quartered (or 1 small can of stewed tomatoes)

8 crushed peppercorns

1 bay leaf

Cook these for five minutes, stirring with a spatula to prevent sticking. Do not let the onions brown! When the vegetables have cooked five or six minutes, season lightly with salt and lay the meat on top of them. Pour over all enough boiling water to almost cover, put on the lid, and simmer gently until the meat is tender — probably in about fifteen to twenty minutes. Add more boiling water if liquid cooks down too much. Serve with crusty sourdough bread to soak up the vegetable sauce.

MESQUITE BAKED CALF'S HEAD

Believe it or not, this is one of *CAD's* most frequently requested recipes. As popular among suburbanites from Scarsdale to Anaheim as it is with Texas ranchers, baked calf's head is a delicacy of the highest order. Not for the faint-hearted and definitely not for those with small appetites, this is the kind of feast that must be cooked in clay soil or sand in order for the fire to get rolling. Note: one calf's head serves eight to ten hungry folks.

Method:

Dig a hole the width and depth of a large garbage can (in clay soil or sand) and build a mesquite log fire in it. When the fire is going good and the flames subside a little, cover the hole with a piece of tin to keep all the fire and heat in the ground. If the fire burns out too rapidly it should be replenished as it takes at least six hours to heat the ground sufficiently. At cooking time the fire is allowed to burn down to ashes and coals.

To prepare the calf's head, remove the hide and wash the oral cavity. Cover it with a layer of heavy paper and then thoroughly wrap it in several wet burlap sacks. Place it in the ashes and coals; cover it completely with coals, hot dirt from the pit, and refill the pit. Put the tin cover on and build a big fire on top of the tin, maintaining the fire until serving time. Cooking is entirely by ground heat and the foregoing process is an all-night or all-day job, the fire being started in proportion to the serving time desired.

To serve, the skull must be cracked open with a cleaver to get at the brains. The latter and the tongue are seasoned with salt, pepper and dried sage — or fresh, if you can get it — to taste. The meat on the outside of the skull needs no seasoning as it is supremely flavorful all on its own.

illustration by Chris Cooper

by Brian M. Chic

The day has been hard, or beautiful, lyrical or brutal. The man has fought, loved, and maybe suffered. All his actions and all their consequences weigh upon him; those which he has calculated and those which he could not foresee. He has misgivings, anguish even. What can bring him back to himself, if only for a moment, but a perfect cigar, the taste of the blue smoke that vanishes into the air like a symbol for the vanity of all undertakings, the precariousness of everything? Nothing or no one else is capable of reconciling him with himself, profoundly, of showing him both the importance of his being and his insignificance in relation to All. — Robert T. Lewis.

Ernie Kovacs, Orson Welles, Groucho Marx ... These are men who most likely will be around forever ... as will their cigars!

Since the mid-1800's, many men of prominence were rarely seen in public (or photographed by Matthew Brady) without their cigars. From the long, thin "cheroots" of Mark Twain to the stubby, half-smoked "stogies" of General Grant, cigar smoking has long since established itself as a novel elegance among personalities whom we may most typify today as "the man's man."

A recognized fashion among English gentlemen of the Edwardian Age, the cigar eventually made its way Westward in time to relieve many of the cumbersome necessities of the pipe. Once a cigar stub was exhausted, it was merely crushed out and tossed aside.

Today, the very presence of a mellow, smoking cigar between the fingers lends immediate prestige to anyone in his latter years, be he statesman or otherwise.

Comedian George Burns (who smokes a very fashionable and private El Producto stock) attests that, while performing, the cigar gives him "time to think" in relation to his inimitable timing. And at its most relaxing, few can deny the pleasure of a good Havanna blend after one's heaviest meal of the day.

Here, then, are just a few helpful tips for the beginning smoker:

SELECTION

In choosing the sort of cigar you'd most like to be associated with, don't betray their purpose by puffing one that makes you sick! Start with a mild "Claro," or light brown tobacco leaf wrapper, of medium length. After awhile, you might try something stronger in a Maduro, or dark brown, wrapper. Then select for yourself.

Cigars with a green wrapper? Don't even think about them.

The next consideration are the fancy names and shapes invading today's cigar market, although most of them are relatively consistent. A Churchill, named after the famous

Prime Minister, is characteristically long, thick, and imposing. It is usually in a Maduro wrapper. When Castro started lighting them up, they went by the term "Presidente."

By contrast, the Rothschild refers to a short, pudgy cigar, popularly sold in both Claro and Maduro wrappers. These are less formal smokes like the earlier mentioned "cheroots." They are easy to carry in the breast pocket of a suit jacket and are often found already half-smoked and clenched between the teeth of bookies, press agents, and house dicks.

But whatever the style, always choose the one which best fits your hand and personality.

LIGHTING AND SMOKING

To determine the crispness and taste beforehand, many a seasoned smoker employs this old tactic:

Gently roll the cigar by your ear between your thumb and middle finger, and then run it lengthwise under your nostrils to inhale the tobacco's bouquet — if it sounds too brittle and smells harsh, you're on your own!

If the "heater" in question is handmade, chances are there will be no hole supplied for intake at the mouth's end. Properly cut your tip, then, with a cigar pierce, guillotine, or "V" cut (most recommended for an easier draw). Crudely biting the tip off and then spitting it in the corner went out of style years ago with Barton MacLane in an endless stream of "B" budget Warner Brothers pictures (also, it'll be sure to queer you with the girls and we certainly wouldn't want that!).

Once you are ready to actually light up, it's a good idea to slowly rotate the cigar in the process while permitting the flame to just barely caress the end. This ensures an even, restful burn.

And whether or not you prefer to believe in the rumor that "butane lighters ruin the taste," one should always try to use a good old-fashioned wooden match (of the household variety) for the dryest and most natural flame.

ETIQUETTE AND STORAGE

While there are "smoking rooms" provided in many of the finer restaurants and theatres, it is always customary for a gentleman to ask "Mind if I smoke?" The delicate noses of some women and older folks may not always be "up to snuff," so the courtesy is appreciated. At any rate, if you

smoke in public, the eyebrows of the opposite sex may rise and take notice if you puff casually, holding the cigar in your hand (and not in your mouth) when not smoking, and assume a confident yet leisurely air.

Consulting your local cigar dealer is practical when seeking an economically satisfactory method of storage. We certainly can't all afford our very own walk-in humidors!

Otherwise, a cigar box or large, plastic container with a resealable lid (like the kind they store food in) is perfect. For an "instant humidor" effect, a small, moist sponge or wad of linen will keep your favorite brand fresh when placed inside. Avoid, also, storing in direct sunlight whenever possible.

Yes, cigar smoking can be suave as well as refreshing. Being a "man of distinction" does not always mean switching to Calvert ... but a good cigar is a smoke!

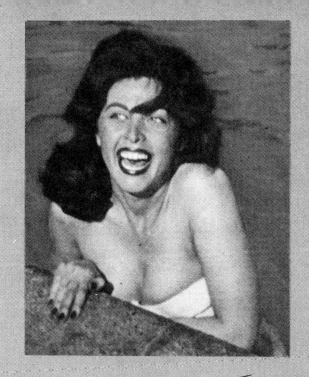
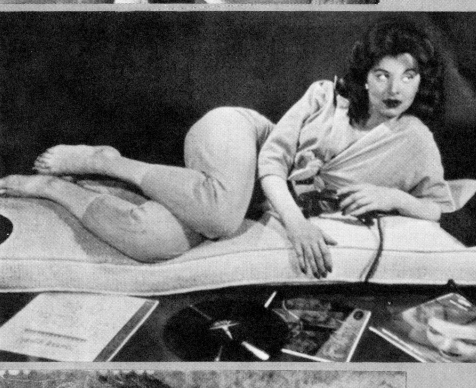

Tina
LOUISE

His rutting and roistering in the gin mills of Papeete was a thing of legend, yet the burdensome task of caring for his senile mother began to smother the spirits of Edgar Leeteg. Long before his black velvet art attracted enough patrons to keep body and soul together, Leeteg dragged mum to his South Sea paradise. Now that he was famous, he often griped about the onslaught of "queers" and "chiselers" arriving in Tahiti to seek him out and sponge off expatriate hospitality. Freebooters had taken over "Villa Velour," his private village on Moorea with a manicured lawn that was as smooth as the imported black velveteen he painted his luminous pictures on. The ten seat Italian marble outhouse, five pastel bungalows, and fabulous circular private cocktail lounge-aquarium overlooking the lush peaks of Paopao Bay had become, in a sense, a jail, where the self-described "fornicating, gin-soaked dopehead, the Moron of Moorea" was a prisoner of his legend and the ill-health of the demanding 77-year-old mother he adored:

Doc from New Zealand bet me a gold cup that I would not make the grade with two strange gals I took in, one from Paris, one from London, who landed here looking for Leeteg. So, Barney, my boy, when you come again next year you can drink your champagne out of a golden goblet! At the moment I have a full house of 25 guests. I have been photographed, put in movies and at

Leeteg of Tahiti

By Charles Krafft

least four of 'em are writing about me. I feel sometimes like blowing this goddamn place up... Tomorrow I'm going to clean house and throw these chiselers out. Godamnit I'm gonna be hard to see from now on: I want to paint and can't with all these people around.

While working as a sign and movie poster painter in Honolulu in the early 1930s, Leeteg met a tattooed submarine sailor named Barney Davis who played the accordion at the Princess Theatre, where Leeteg's company had its offices. Fifteen years after their first meeting, Davis opened a Honolulu art shop where he sold his first Leetegs for $135 each. In a few short years, the Davis Art Gallery was selling original Leeteg velvets for $7,000 to $10,000, a hefty sum for the early 1950s. The business relationship was notable for two reasons. Davis sent huge sums of money to Leeteg in Tahiti, and Leeteg in return sent Davis long letters in which the most intimate aspects of his flammable life in French Oceania were discussed. These two hard-drinking vagabonds singlehandedly created a legend and an art tradition that has become synonymous with tourism today from Tijuana to Timbuktu:

Please don't bother submitting any of my work to art societies or museums as I hold them long haired bastards in contempt since I know alot about how they operate. Leave them to plug their own darling daubers. We don't need them and they're just cheap four-flushers in frock coats. Tell them Leeteg is very particular about hanging his pictures with some of the stuff that is now classed as art...

Before entering into this lucrative partnership, Leeteg us selling or trading his velvets for whatever he could get. was Barney Davis' free use of the names Rembrandt, ls, and Rubens that convinced his customers to accept the er-increasing prices he put on the paintings of this American Gauguin." The artist's years of reckless exhibinism on his regular crawls through the grog shops and orehouses of Papeete had already made him a highly visie and unpopular social scourge in the tiny Anglo-French-inese colony. No doubt much of the carefree, riotous, colful glamour with which the world associates Tahiti was e result of stories about Leeteg's debauches circulated hong sailors. It was a sailor who originally pestered Davis to acquiring a velvet hanging in a rugged Honolulu bar eteg had once traded for drinks and sandwiches. Davis d lost sight of Leeteg years earlier and wasn't aware he inted anything but signs. When a Mormon missionary turning from Tahiti wandered into Davis' shop bearing o velvets, he immediately rushed off an air mail letter and 00 with instructions for Leeteg to send regular shipments his work.

By this time Leeteg had already put fourteen years into rfecting the secret technique that would resurrect and revize the centuries old art of painting on velvet. He had also cked up a patron in the form of a genial Salt Lake City weler named Wayne Decker. Decker's standing order: end us one of everything you paint," had provided funds r the house on Moorea Leeteg built for his mother and mself. The Deckers had also sent money when Mama rtha Leeteg was forced to travel to Hawaii to recouperate om a near fatal illness. Despite his stipend, Leeteg was rely scraping by when Davis tracked him down. His boisrous parties and a fantastic building program which outged neighbor Richard Gump (the genteel head of Gump's San Francisco) provoked epic battles with Tahitians and uropeans alike. The entire colony was set agog when Davis ally arrived in 1952 and announced flatly that the bane of eir propriety was as great as Rembrandt and the hottest lling artist of modern times.

Controversy followed Leeteg everywhere, but there had en a technical problem to overcome before Barney Davis uld parley the volatile artist's notoriety into international me and fortune. French and American customs officials aimed that his velvets were not art. In defense of his right enter his work into the United States duty free, instead of der heavy charges as mass-produced artisan's work,

Willis Shook, of the Art Institute of Pittsburgh, was enlisted to justify Leeteg's technique:

I sat beside him and watched him begin, develop, and complete several paintings. I am quite willing to state under oath that he draws the figures from life, freehand, paints them in exactly as does any artist producing work that is called 'fine art'. He uses no mechanical aids whatever in the production of his paintings, neither airbrush, stencil, reflector, projector, nor any other means other that his eye and hand. I have seen no such magnificent effect in any other artist's work.

Leeteg's financial prolifigacy prior to Davis' sensationally earnest promotions kept him struggling for years to make ends meet. Besides his mother, he supported two "official" Tahitian wives who had borne him three children, as well as countless native models, mistresses and local madames who had come and gone. The artist-mother-sweetheart tensions never eased at the "Villa Velour" and were compounded by both the Leeteg's refusal to avail themselves of the lush bounty of abundant tropical fruits and fish all around them. They subsisted exclusively on imported tinned goods bought at great expense from the Chinese merchants in Papeete. Mama Leeteg's inflexible domination drove away all 14 of his Tahitian "wives," just as she's succeeded in breaking up her son's two previous American marriages.

As Leeteg's fortunes increased, so did his frustrations and inner conflicts. His erratic behavior was the result of problems he could not solve and from which he tried unsuccessfully to escape. As these grew more acute, he could not endure his own company and compulsively looked to the boozy night life of Papeete for temporary distraction. On Tuesday of every week he would visit Papeete by public motor launch and spend a day and a night carousing and brawling. On Wednesday morning he would return on the "Mitiaro" to Moorea to recover, paint more pictures, and prepare for another assault on Papeete:

You tell me to go easy on the bottle and get down to work. Are you beginning to believe that stuff about me being an alkie? Which I appear to be for the benefit of the tourists. What the tourists don't see is me hard at work before my easel six days a week every week including Sundays ... Getting plenty choice stuff these days ... I feel like a nigger in a watermelon patch among all these hot mamas. Also this is my favorite way of spending money. It's worth every cent usually!!!

At the height of his career Leeteg was producing a painting every four days. It took him up to three weeks to finish each velvet, carrying forward as many as a half dozen at once to keep up with the demand. His pioneering technique that launched and army of imitators

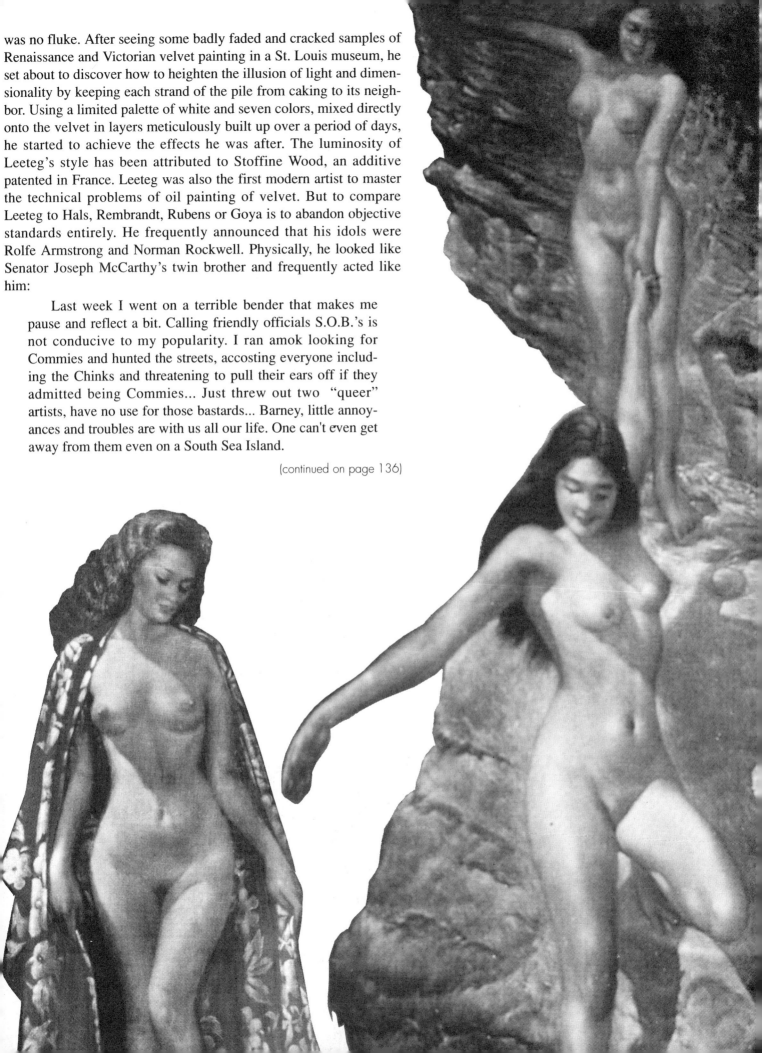

was no fluke. After seeing some badly faded and cracked samples of Renaissance and Victorian velvet painting in a St. Louis museum, he set about to discover how to heighten the illusion of light and dimensionality by keeping each strand of the pile from caking to its neighbor. Using a limited palette of white and seven colors, mixed directly onto the velvet in layers meticulously built up over a period of days, he started to achieve the effects he was after. The luminosity of Leeteg's style has been attributed to Stoffine Wood, an additive patented in France. Leeteg was also the first modern artist to master the technical problems of oil painting of velvet. But to compare Leeteg to Hals, Rembrandt, Rubens or Goya is to abandon objective standards entirely. He frequently announced that his idols were Rolfe Armstrong and Norman Rockwell. Physically, he looked like Senator Joseph McCarthy's twin brother and frequently acted like him:

Last week I went on a terrible bender that makes me pause and reflect a bit. Calling friendly officials S.O.B.'s is not conducive to my popularity. I ran amok looking for Commies and hunted the streets, accosting everyone including the Chinks and threatening to pull their ears off if they admitted being Commies... Just threw out two "queer" artists, have no use for those bastards... Barney, little annoyances and troubles are with us all our life. One can't even get away from them even on a South Sea Island.

(continued on page 136)

Ode on Masculine Independence

It's quite a fight
To be a cenobite.
Misogynistic,
Or merely mystic,
Find it unmerry
In a monastery,
But — if you need a woman —
Turn atavistic!

Follow the trail
Of some female,
Hale
Her by the hair
To your horrid lair,
Slap her into a chair,
Say, "Sit there!
Don't always be needing
To fix your hair!
Stop reading!
Stop shopwalking!
Stop prating!
Don't keep me waiting!
Stop prinking!
Yes, and *stop thinking!*
Don't always be talking
When I want to talk!
Don't always be eating!
You need a beating!"

To the tyrannosaurus and the auk,
Brothers, let us revert—-
To telling Them things that hurt,
To being thoroughly annoying,

To enjoying
With cruel chaff
And a sneering laugh
Their plaintive squawk —
Gosh, yes! —
To positive battening
On their distress.
That would be fattening,
That would be swell —
To tell
Them impolitely
But quite rightly
To go to hell —
For every foible, fad, and whim,
To make 'em crawl out on a limb,
And shake 'em off in a pool in which they couldn't swim!
O then like bullfrogs we'd swell out chests,
Then like gorillas we'd beat our breasts,
Then we'd be
The dominant He —
Not the subservient Him!

... Hello? What's that, darling? Oh, just writing something ... No, nothing important ... Well, of course, I did rather want this evening ... Oh, no, darling, it's really quite all right if you want us to go. I don't suppose we have to dress ... Oh, I only meant, darling ... Oh, of course it's all right if it's going to be so formal ... Yes, certainly I'll hurry ... Now, now, darling, you know I'm always on time ... Yes, certainly, dear ... Oh, by all means! ... Oh, you'r quite right! Yes, yes, certainly, darling....
— William Rose Benet

Clyde Stanley

CAD'S GALLERY

Cat Girl

Lilly (THE CAT GIRL) Christine is a lot of woman. Particularly because a lot of people think so. Particularly men. Natch. Called America's greatest Bellyrina, Lilly has starred in Michael Todd's Broadway musical — *Peep Show* and *Strip For Action;* she's also the pinup darling of

countless college dorms and GI barracks walls throughout the world. She has that indefinable something that every gal in show business hopes for — sex appeal. With Lilly the talent comes naturally.

What does she think about men? We interviewed for for CAD, and this is what she says:

"My weakness is a man who's all man. I melt to a sexy masculine voice — tall, rangy, wide shoulders, athletic — a little rough, a little demanding, but with enough sensitivity to smooth the edges. GIs and college boys are my pet 'Bob Cats' for they are refreshingly athletic, interesting with a good sense of humor."

"Given half a chance our American males are wonderfully, poetically romantic. But it's the woman's job to create a romantic atmosphere to encourage him to show that side of his nature."

"The only thing I find wrong about American men is that they are inclined to be extravagant. A guy seems to think he must impress a girl, particularly on a first date. He selects a very expensive restaurant, the most costly play in town, or glittering nightclub. Usually he can't afford all this so his next date with the girl may be delayed until he can afford another lush evening. The fact is most girls will be happier over a hamburger and a trip to the beach. A girl wants to get to know a fellow. That's the important thing."

Lilly, CAD hereby votes you the gal we'd most like to share a hamburger with.

What follows, dear reader, is the uncensored version of that original ballad of YOUNG LUST exactly as it was told on the streets of Harlem in the 1900's. Now you'll know why wandering balladeers were arrested for singing what you thought was an 'old standard'...

FRaNKie aND JOHNNie

Illustrated by KLOWES
Lyrics reprinted from THE IMMORTALIA ©1927

Frankie and Johnnie were lovers:
   Goodness, Oh God! How they'd love—
Swore to be true to each other,
   True as the stars above.
For he was her man,
   But he done her wrong! .

Frankie was a good girl,
   Most everybody knows,
She gave a hundred dollars
   To Johnnie for a suit of clothes.
Cause he was her man,
   But he done her wrong!

Frankie worked in a crib-joint,
   A place that's got two doors;
Gave all her money to Johnnie,
   Who spent it on parlor-house whores.
God-damn his soul,
   He done her wrong!

Frankie was a fucky hussy—
   That's what all the pricks said—
And they kept her so damn busy,
   She never had time to get out of bed.
But he done her wrong,
   God-damn his soul!

Frankie hung a sign on her door,
   "No more fish for sale."
Then she went looking for Johnnie
   To give him all her kale.
He was a-doin' her wrong,
   God-damn his soul!

Frankie went down Fourth Street
  To get a glass of steam-beer;
Said to the man called bartender,
  "Has my lovin' Johnnie been here?
God-damn his soul,
  He's a-doin' me wrong!"

"I couldn't tell you no story,
  I couldn't tell you no lie,
I saw your Johnnie an hour ago
  With a coon called Alice Bly.
God-damn his soul,
  He was a-doin' you wrong!"

Frankie ran back to the crib-joint,
  Took the oilcloth off the bed,
Took out a bindle of coke
  And snuffed it right up in her head;
God-damn his soul,
  He was a-doin' her wrong!

Then she put on her red kimona,
  This time it wasn't for fun;
Cause right underneath it
  Was a great big forty-four gun.
She went huntin' her man,
  Who was a-doin' her wrong!

She ran along Fish Alley,
  And looked in a window high,
And she saw her lovin' Johnnie
  Finger-frigging Alice Bly.
He was a-doin' her wrong,
  God-damn his soul!

Frankie went to the hop-joint,
  Frankie rang the hop-joint bell:
"Stand back you pimps and whores,
  Or I'll blow you straight to hell.
I'm huntin' my man,
  Who's a-doin' me wrong!"

Frankie ran up the stairway—
    Johnnie hollered, "Please don't shoot!"
But Frankie raised the forty-four
    And went five times, root-ti-toot.
She shot her man,
    'Cause he done her wrong!

"Turn me over Frankie,
    Turn me over slow;
A bullet got me on my right side,
    Oh Gawd! It hurts me so.
You've killed your man,
    But I done you wrong!"

Then came the scene in the courthouse:
    Frankie said, as bold as brass,
"Judge, I didn't shoot him in the third degree,
    I shot him in his big fat ass;
'Cause he was my man,
    An' was a-doin' me wrong!"

Bring out your rubber-tired hearse.
    Bring out your rubber-tired hacks.
Hearse to take Johnnie to the cemetery;
    Hacks to bring all the whores back:
For he's dead and gone,
    'Cause he done her wrong!

The sergeant said to Frankie,
    "It may all be for the best,
He always chased 'round parlor-house whores,
    He sure was an awful pest;
Now he's dead and gone,
    He was a-doin' you wrong!"

Three little pieces of crepe
    Hanging on the crib-joint door,
Signifies that Johnnie
    Will never be a pimp no more.
God-damn his soul,
    He done her wrong!

Mrs. Hanson's

He stood looking at the pleading flesh for a long moment, then tried to break the chains with his hands.

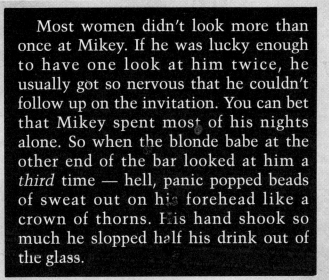

Most women didn't look more than once at Mikey. If he was lucky enough to have one look at him twice, he usually got so nervous that he couldn't follow up on the invitation. You can bet that Mikey spent most of his nights alone. So when the blonde babe at the other end of the bar looked at him a *third* time — hell, panic popped beads of sweat out on his forehead like a crown of thorns. His hand shook so much he slopped half his drink out of the glass.

Secret

BY E. Peter Regis

She wouldn't look away, either. Mikey would look away, then glance back to find that she was still watching him. He had a lot of trouble getting the cigarette to his mouth. Her eyes smouldered out of an oval-cut face with high cheekbones. She gave him a lazy smile then ran a slow, pink tongue over

(continued on page 137)

There's no mistaking a Russ Meyer movie. Big, bold, bouncy, Meyer's films combine technical expertise with a sharp sense of humor and a glorious obsession for, shall we say, overendowed women. "Ladies with large breastworks," as Russ himself might put it. The kind men like.

Meyer's home in the Hollywood Hills is painted an electrifying green and orange, trimmed with yellow. Inside, every available inch of wall and ceiling space is covered with mementos, pictures and posters, almost all of them featuring females with knock-out knockers. From snapshots to larger-than-life movie posters, there are stupendous breasts everywhere the eye looks. The very air abounds in bosoms.

The Grand Titmeister himself talks freely and without hesitation, keeping nothing hidden. He enjoys telling a good story, and he has almost as many of them as he does photos of breasts.

This interview was conducted over two evenings by Sergei Hasenecz and Charles Schneider.

Let's talk about your film work first. Which filmmakers were an influence on you?

Nobody.

No one at all?

No one's been an influence whatsoever. My films are so Russ Meyer, you know? No one makes a better Russ Meyer movie than Russ Meyer. I just had my hang-ups, as you know. Big tits. I certainly didn't have any difficulty in encouraging myself to admire women with large overbites. I would say that I had a perfectly clear-cut course, once I got out of the service, as to what I wanted to do, and that was certainly to be in film.

But in the beginning I was really put down by the majors [studios]. I got out of the service thinking that I might handily get a job, like assistant cameraman or filmloader. Turned down, understandably. They had a lot of people that had previously been employed, you know, and when you came back from the service that was the rule: give them their jobs. Fine. It was probably the best thing that happened to me because I didn't have to work my way up the ladder. I was very fortunate to be introduced by a letter to a gentleman in San Francisco. His name was Gene Walker, an industrial filmmaker. He had a number of interesting clients. Southern Pacific, Standard Oil, and Zellerbach Paper.

Working for them and his films gave me the opportunity to shoot thousands of feet of film under all kinds of circumstances. And learn about script writing, although these were documentaries. Their impact is very much felt on my films, because my films do have kind of a documentary feel to them, with a narrator and things of that nature.

So, your editing style and camera technique are self-taught?

Oh, absolutely. I'm not influenced by a soul. In fact, I so seldom go to movies. I'm really not interested in going to them. Not that I feel that I'll be, you know, tainted by it. I'll go to see Eastwood's movies, by and large, because I like gut-pulling movies. Really violent pictures. Not horror films, but really violent pictures. My violence is jokey and overdone. I like the old noir films. Victor Mature and Dick Powell. Mitchum. I had my sights set pretty clearly in the beginning, and I enjoyed being in the company of outrageously abundant ladies. I was in a position to photograph them, or marry them, or live with them, and get their pictures published in magazines.

And when it came time to get back into making some sort of sex film, I had the pleasure of knowing a man by the name of Peter De Cenzie. He was the last burlesque entrepreneur on the West Coast. Remarkable man. He was the guy who brought Tempest Storm to the fore, and Lili St. Cyr. And then things went poor for him politically in Oakland. They got him by

HERE WE GO AGAIN, BOYS!

Eve AND THE HANDYMAN

ANOTHER RIOT OF VOLUPTUOUS LAUGHS BY THE PRODUCER OF — "THE IMMORAL MR. TEAS"

A SHOWER OF VOLUPTUOUS LAUGHS & SEX!
STARRING
EVE MEYER and ANTHONY-JAMES RYAN

IN BLUSHING, RIOTOUS EASTMAN COLOR

FOR THE BROAD-MINDED ADULT ONLY

IT'S LOADED WITH BELLY LAUGHS AND NATURAL BARE HUMOR

. . A thick-set, mustachioed hulk sounding off/hunker'd down over a 35mm Arri BL motion picture camera/two assistants at the ready . . one reed-thin standing by with a clapper slate; the other close-knit . . knees akimbo/directing the Sennheiser shotgun mike and at his feet a Nagra Mark IV sound recorder. The camera's subject from nearby Atlanta and a legend hereabouts, almost indescribable in configuration . . overwhelmingly stacked/protuberant abbondanza . . a cantilevered powerhouse of scrotum-busting/first strike capability! A numbing undulatory presence perched high atop a Georgia peach tree . . recumbent/supine upon Alabama's St. Augustine sod . . to rollick/gambol atop New Mexico's many splendor'd lofty deserts . . prostrate/spread-eagled in Texas' tallest tavern . . wherever, the bearish one gruntingly extolling/ entreating/exorcising/extracting/ eulogizing . . compliments heaped upon the superlative/adjective atop adverb . . a salivating/melon-breasted/adumbrating salient swaying/upsurging-in-place . . her lyre-like hips gyrating in ever-widening circles, a washboard-flat pelvis festooned by a luxuriously hairy/soft underbelly . . seemingly aflow therein, with an overlarge/exquisite golden lavaliere rhythmically disappearing/embosomed . . heroically reappearing from a depth/deep within a cavernous valley . . scarcely discernible whilst stubbornly cleaving a set of colossal/really humongous mind-blowing tits!

— Russ Meyer
A Clean Breast: The Life and Loves of Russ Meyer

the shorthairs and took his theater away from him. So, he'd always been after me to make a film having to do with nudity. His taste was rather simple. Had to do with volleyball and croquet and nudists. I had been doing some work for Playboy at that time. "The Girl Next Door," these kind of stories. I couldn't handle a nudist film, but nevertheless, that's how *Teas* [*The Immoral Mr. Teas*] came about.

I had an idea . . I'd been doing something with Bill Teas. He was an army friend of mine, a photographer. I presented the idea to Pete that we'd do a film about a man who hallucinates and can see a girl without her clothing. He produced the film on the basis of it being kind of a documentary. Narrator commenting on today's hustle and bustle in the city. And it worked out fine. So anyway, that's how it all started. Preoccupation with tits. Still have it. Love 'em. Go out of my way to be with somebody that's new, that's built like a brick shithouse.

For this interview, we had considered finding the most magnificently buxom woman possible, hang a little Brownie camera between her breasts and say to you, "We brought a photographer. We hope you don't mind."

It's hard to find a buxom woman. I don't know. [chuckles] That's very good, though.

You said that the title CAD: A Handbook for Heels *somehow applied to you. In what way?*

I've been a shit more than once, twice in my life. I've been not altogether the most responsible person when it came to women that I knew. I was prone to move along and seek

some other kind of companionship. Another lady, for example. A number of things I've done in my life wasn't altogether that, shall I say, honorable. And it bugs me every now and then when I think about it. But on the other hand one has to always seek his own pleasures and live by his own tastes and devil take the breastmost.

We had to ask this question, the classic Sigmund Freud question: "What does a woman want?" Do you have any ideas?

Meyer's first lay, as drawn by Bill Ward

What does what?

"What does a woman want?"

Depends on the woman. [Indicates a picture of actress and ex-wife Edy Williams.] Now Miss Williams would like an unlimited amount of money. And just to lather and layer it upon her. She was my third wife. Eve, who was my second wife, and one of the seven great women in my life too, was a marvelous lady and very dedicated. Anxious to help. What did she want? She wanted to have a child. She couldn't have a child, so . . And that always bugged her, of course. Regrettably, our marriage did an el foldo after about nine years. I was able to really remain faithful to her for that number of years, which is remarkable. [Indicates Eve Meyer's picture.] Great head on this lady.

And there have been ladies like Uschi Digard, who's been very special to me. Or Kitten Natividad. We've been together on and off for many years. So she's very special to me. In an all-around way, the two women that have done the most for me is Eve and Kitten. Whether it be sexual or just the companionship, camaraderie, the concern, the well-being, the works. But there are others that are not too far behind. Uschi Digard. Rena Horton. They're special ladies. And then I've known a number of them. One I can't name, but I call her "Miss Mattress." She's married and she's totally devoted to fucking. And there's another lady by the name of Janet Buxton, which I handle very accurately and straightforwardly in my book [Meyer's forthcoming autobiography, *A Clean Breast, The Life and Loves of Russ Meyer*], who is also in that area. Married and dedicated to screwing. Robustuous low body blows!

I think that's one of the things about the book that would be interesting, is that most film books are books that don't sell very well. They just have a little following, people buy so many. Well, it's a combination of the life and loves of Russ Meyer. Told very frankly, humorously, nothing negative. And I've been able to write very well about that. And I think that in itself is worth the price of the book. But then also we'll have twenty-three hundred pictures, and opposite of each page of text we will have pictures that have direct relationship to what you're reading. It'll be eleven and a half pounds and two volumes. [The book has since reached three volumes.] Nine by twelve.

Yea, we got a lot of orders already. The book is going to sell for an outrageous amount of money. I have about two dozen people that will get a free copy. No one else will. The press will pay for it, but they will pay for it at cost. And the check will be made out to the Sloane-Kettering Cancer Institute. The rest of the five thousand [copies] have been pretty much sold already, and that will be it. And then we may go for another five thousand. I think it's going to be a very big seller. Even at the steep price, people are sending in their money. But a long time ago I made up my mind that I would not dole this out to the press, under any circumstance. If they're going to give me a bad review, they're going to have to pay. I think it's an interesting and also very positive way of dealing with the press.

I've done the book over and over, and each time another adverb, another adjective, and it's better. It's written like the old Spicy Mystery books. The girls that I've had anything personal with, our conversations and the noises. The whole works are in here. You sleep with a synonym book. You come up with words and I don't care if some people don't understand what the damn word means. Or I manufacture words. For breasts: *abbondanzas*, giganzos, big overbite, large balcony!

How many different words are there?

Oh, I've got it all. Rib rack, bellings, bristols, boondogglers, etc. You know. It's all there. But always preceded by large/gigantic/immense/huge/Atlantean/cyclopean/whopping/Brobdingnagian/humongous!

Instead of a footnote, you'll have a titnote, if it has some specific reference to tits. It's bound to give me a lot of credibility. It's racy as hell, it's descriptive, it's florid. Those magazines just went so far. This does the whole thing. There's a lot of manufactured words in there, emotions, like "aaargh!" and "woo-eey!" Great-grandfather grandmother fucking. That kind of good stuff. It works. I think that the Collins sisters, Sidney Sheldon can get out of the business. They don't begin to write nearly as well as I do about jokey sex. But it was laborious, it was not easy. Over and over. What words to italicize. Picking out one word to emphasize.

Do you write by hand?

On yellow tablets. I have never been mechanical enough ... The feeling of a pencil.

How did you come up with the title Faster Pussycat, Kill! Kill! *(1966)?*

The man was here just before you came. He's a sound effects editor, worked with me on a lot of pictures. He came up with the title. His name's Dick Brummer. We had thought about "The Leather Girls," things like that. He came over one morning. We were working on the picture doing the editing. He says, "I've got a title. You've got to listen to it. 'Faster Pussycat, Kill! Kill!'" I said, "Wow!"

Our readers are going to want to know, what's the best pick-up line you've ever heard?

Pick-up line ... You mean some kind of saying —

There's a woman and you want to go to bed with her —

Haji, Loni Williams, Tura Satana in *Faster Pussycat, Kill! Kill!*

Sheri Knight in *Erotica*

Oh, you mean to pick her up? Oh, I don't believe in that. I've been able to meet women on the basis of my business. I get to know them on a professional level and if I feel there's some sort of interest on their part, as well as mine, because no one likes to be turned down. But it's not done some smarmy-assed way. They can tell I care for them, pretty much so.

Do you have a preference between blondes or brunettes or redheads?

No, no. My preference is big tits and that's it. Plain and simple.

Does it matter to you if tits are naturally large or implanted? Does that make a difference?

That makes no difference because they make them now so wonderful. That's one thing about [stripper and model] Melissa Mounds. When I first met her, she said, "Now take hold and feel these tits. This is why I'm a success." Sure, they're augmented. But you can sink your fingers in and you can't find any foreign substance.

And nipples, is there a particular aesthetic —?

No. I don't like, you know, the big brown jobs. Kitten has very petite nipples but huge tits.

What was your first girlfriend like?

The first woman I ever had? Ernest Hemingway got her for me. The first chick I ever had, she was 21 years old and in a whorehouse. I ran into Hemingway's lieutenant, who was a Portuguese gentleman. Hemingway was in this town outside

of Paris and was instrumental in getting us into a whorehouse that had been closed down because the currency hadn't been established. The Germans had left and now the Americans were coming in. We were the only Americans in town, so it was quite an experience. And right off the bat, the girl of my dreams. [Indicates a picture of a Meyeresque lady.] She was built like that, the one I selected. So Hemingway did a good deed for me.

There are a number of your films with hookers as characters. Does this come from any other personal experience?

Hookers are great ladies, as far as I'm concerned. "Finders Keepers" [*Finders Keepers, Lovers Weepers* (1968)] had a couple of hookers in it. Claire, who was the black madame, and Christina, I guess it was, played by Jan Sinclair, had beautiful conical tits. She was supposedly a specialty hooker. I can't think of any other that had hookers, right off the top of my head.

Mudhoney (1965).

Oh, of course. Very important. They were the bucolic hookers. Yeah. Thank you. Rena Horton and Lorna Maitland.

What is your all-time favorite strip joint, the finest you've ever seen?

When I was in the army I had a week off from basic training. My mates had come from Southern California, I came from Northern California. I got there before them, so I was able to be given a week off and I went to Kansas City. Kansas City always had a very good burlesque there, and they just recently reconditioned it. It's now become a very fancy stage theater. That was the KC Follies. It was built in the tradition of tall ceilings and balconies and boxes. You could get way up close to the stage and look down on the girls.

I went to this theater and I saw a girl who had been a former Miss St. Louis. She tried to qualify in the Miss America contest. Why she didn't win, I don't know. I guess her tits were too big. And God, she was just ... just an elegant girl. All I could do was go and see her every day on the stage, 'cause I was so taken by her. But I did not have the knowledge, the wherewithal, I just didn't feel adequate to go after a chick like this who was the headliner. It wasn't until after the war. Two, three years after the war, I guess it was. I had been working on these industri-

al films, and I encountered an advertisement in a page of the *LA Times*. And here it was the same girl from St. Louis appearing at the Burbank Follies. These kind of theaters are no longer in existence. Beautiful, beautiful theaters. The star of the show was something else, too. Miss St. Louis. I don't use her name because I speak frankly about her in my book and you never know how they'll feel about that. I had the good fortune of seeing her ad in the paper. I got my ass down there.

So I went in and sure it was, the same chick with the pointy tits and the pageboy hairdo. God, and I was just really excited and nervous. I said, I'm going to meet her somehow and take some pictures of her or whatever. I tried to figure it out. Those girls are notoriously suspicious 'cause everybody's hitting on them. So I went back and I had it all planned. I went to the green room, they call it, and give 'em my card. I said, "There's a comic back there I want to talk to." 'Cause the comic had done a film for De Cenzie in the beginning called *French Peep Show* (1950) before I did "Mr. Teas." I was the camerman and director.

This puzzled the doorkeep because, God, no one ever asked for a comic. So I knew exactly what I was going to do. I had to get a friend in the court, see? So the comic came out and we had a nice little chat, and I say, "Hey, do me a favor. You know, there's a girl back there I'd like to photograph. You think you could

Roger Ebert &

42

bring her out?" "Yea sure, I think so." You see it was much easier to have someone else do the heavy work. You asked about picking somebody up, see? So he went in, brought her out.

She was pleasant as hell. I said, I want some photographs. I told her I do stuff for magazines and such. "Oh, OK. How about tomorrow night?" I said, "No, no, I have to do it tonight because I'm going home to Frisco." She said okay. So I took a lot of pictures of her. So then we were over with her mother. Sent some pictures to her. Appreciated it very much. She says, next time you're down, give me a call. So, that was it. That's how we got started. We ended up on Mulholland Drive, whaling away. There was no hanky-panky bullshit about trying to con somebody. She liked the way I delivered, as it were. I delivered her some pictures. It was great.

What was it like taking pictures for those great men's magazines?

Well, Eve and I, we did it exclusively for quite some time, for about a year. It was so good for our marriage, because we'd be shooting, I'd get a hard-on and just lay her down and [claps hands] on the floor, you know, whale away. Then she'd get it all straightened out and take some more pictures. And of all the ladies I ever met, that was it. We were married, it was great, and we always had nice encounters. We cared for one another. She'd get me

Russ Meyer

up, and she'd get wet [claps hands] and that's the way.

How did you meet Eve?

She was a legal secretary in San Francisco, and her name was bandied about by the lawyer who supervised my divorce from my first wife. We were in this place called The Blackhawk, a jazz club, and ran into this lawyer who was three sheets to the wind. He said, hey, there's this great girl, blonde goddess, and blah blah blah. He gave her card to a friend of mine who was an Eastman Kodak tech rep named Ray Grant, who's the one that really made it possible for *Mr. Teas* to get processed. Put his job on the line. An experiment in wet gate blow-ups. You know, 16 to 35mm. So he gave me the card. He said, "I can't have this card. My old lady will find it." So I kept it for a month and then I called her. And she was really pissed at me.

Anyway, we got together. We were very close. We married and then we did a lot of work together. For example, some of those photographs [indicates late '50s men's magazine] which I treasure so much. She became a national institution. She was really well-endowed as a model, and we sold a lot of pictures and made a lot of money. She got to a point where she would become disenchanted with it, but I could always talk her into doing something. Which is great for a man and woman to have that kind of personal turn-on.

And then I made the first film. She didn't feel like she was really a part of the whole thing. But then finally she was in charge of distribution. She always locked horns to horns with my partner De Cenzie. She had a gung-ho attitude. She knew how to handle these not-altogether-that-honest distributors. And besides, the nifty breastworks. So we had a great marriage, I guess about eight years, and then it started to fall apart. For a number of reasons. And then she, regrettably, was killed in an airplane crash. Down in Tenerife. Two big jumbo jets. So she has to be one of the more important women in my life.

I showed *Pussycat* and *Beneath the Valley of the Ultra Vixens* (1979) at a film festival in San Jose. And two nice newspaper men did good pieces. It was important to me to go because my mother was born in that town. That was the only reason I went. One of the writers, his name was [Richard] von Busack, he saw me to

Babette Bardot in *Common-Law Cabin*

the door, and I was going to have a late dinner with a friend of mine. I trudged off into the night, carrying a can of film, which is pretty heavy, and Busack says, "I couldn't help but notice you when you walked off. And I said to myself, 'There goes a legend.'" You remember Jimmy Durante? He had that Calabash thing. On television. "Good night, Mrs. Calabash." And he walked off. I likened it to something like that. Probably so. Could be.

Quite a compliment.

I was telling Kitten about the name of your book, and she said, "Perfect. [Laughs.] Perfect title for you. Cad." It's true. I started thinking about your thing about the business of being a cad. A cad, by and large, is someone who kind of ... He could do a number of things. Shunt a woman aside after she's given her best, as it were. Right? Abandoning her. Forcing her into an abortion. Becoming disenchanted with her most personal place plus her most personal tits. Looking for somebody bigger. That's me. That's exactly me. I've done it all my life.

I think there are as many women, or even more so, women that I have known in my time, that I really couldn't go up to and say "Hi," because I'd probably be struck. Or there would be some terrible blasphemy that would come out of their lips. Or they might even stand there and cry, would make you feel even worse. Much better to be kicked in the balls. And I've been part and parcel to this, part and party. And it awakened the fact — which I have been documenting in my book, very straightforwardly — always, you know, looking for a bigger pair of tits. I wouldn't be a bit surprised if a large share of them would think very ill of me. Very definitely. I think that's one of the things I've made very clear in my book, and I've told it very accurately. But on the other hand I've always said to myself, that if you're not happy, they won't be happy. So what are you going to do? There are guys who place themselves in purgatory for their entire lives and never take a shot at something a little out of the ordinary. So, it's not all bad to be bad.

And without a doubt, a cad is a man who loves women.

Well, for a while.

For a while?

That's right. Love is a very intangible thing. Kitten and I have been lovers for years. And she needs some help now, some real friendship, aside from, you know, just bellying-it-up-to and so on. I just feel kind of an obligation to help her a little more.

My mother really represents my most important person. And two of the women displayed a lot of affection for her. I mean, they did it at a time when she was not her brightest. If they'd done it when she was sharp, she'd have probably said, "What does she want from me?" You know? But both of them, Uschi Digard and Kitten Natividad, would attend to her in so many ways. Particularly, Kitten would take a bunch of strippers over to the old ladies home — that's a terrible way of putting it. The rest

Raven De La Croix in *Up!*

home, that's what it's called. There were men there as well.— and they'd dance for the women and the men. They wouldn't be unclothed, but these four or five strippers would go over there with Kitten Natividad. The women would clap. And you'd wonder if they ever knew what these girls were doing. I'm putting it like, [ominous] "What were they doing, these unchaste women?" Which is far from the truth. Nevertheless, I couldn't help but feel a great empathy for those two ladies in particular, the way they did indeed show my mother a lot of consideration. She was sick and infirm and old.

Particularly if you have a circle of friends that are all pretty much the same age, such as I have, and they are ... starting to go. Anyways, that's maudlin. Go ahead. Back to tits.

A slight detour from tits to your filmwork, although we really can't separate them. We were wondering how much pre-planning you do before shooting. Do you make storyboards or do you shoot from the hip?

No, I know what it's all about. First of all, I, by and large, always do the treatment. It's my story. The treatment is based upon a location. Do it in reverse. Before getting the idea, I find the location. And then I fit the location onto the script. The location is generally always some woebegone area. I mean, it's really the swamps, terrible cruel desert, things like that. Then I do the treatment. And then either I involve a writer with me, or in some instances I do it entirely by myself. [Film critic Roger] Ebert participated in four screenplays.

Four?

Four. Yea. Three of them were under pseudonyms. The first one was *Beyond the Valley of the Dolls* (1970). That was [20th Century] Fox. Later he felt that he should use a pseudonym because he started getting work as a reviewer on television, it would be more to his advantage to use a pseudonym. Which was okay by me. But when he did "Dolls" he caught hell from his peers. Fortunately he survived and now he's openly admitting to being a participant. I mean, on national shows. For *Beneath the Valley of the Ultravixens* and *Up!* (1976) he used the name "R. Hyde," as in Dr. Jekyll and Roger Hyde. And another was a good one, "Rheinhold Timme," a man I met in Berlin. I don't recall the other one. It was kind of a WC Fields connotation.

Back to the idea. The idea's mine. Someone, or myself, or both of us write the script. And then I go about casting the film, which is the nastiest part of all. It is so frustrating to try and cast a Russ Meyer movie, simply because there are not many women like that around, and you are always lucky just to find one. In the case of *Lorna* (1964) for example, I couldn't even find the girl that I wanted. We'd even selected and given the part to somebody, and at the last moment this other girl came forward. Lorna Maitland. And we had to pay off the other girl and use Lorna. You know, I just didn't feel that kind of solid feeling that I normally feel when I cast a picture.

Curiously, in *Supervixens* (1975) I got lucky. I found six girls, six supergirls, but we couldn't find the seventh. There was some thought at the time that Edy Williams might do it, which she would liked to have done. But to work with her, the wife, it would never have worked. She would have ended up trying to direct the movie.

I'll never forget. Charles Napier, he had already done *Cherry, Harry & Raquel* (1969). We met out in — he loves redneck areas — a redneck bar. I was lamenting about the casting. He knew he was cast and all that. He was anxious, gung-ho to get going. And he said to me, "We're held up by this super angel broad?" I said, "Yea, I just can't find her." So he said, "How about Edy?" I had mentioned something to Edy, about Napier's a good actor and so forth, and if I do another film I'm certainly going to use him. Napier said, "She's beautiful. No question about that." She had worked in a film with him. He had been in *Seven Minutes* (1971) and *Beyond the Valley of the Dolls.* And then she said, "Why would you give a man so many lines in a film? They want to look at my beautiful body." So I told him that. He said, "The cunt!" [Laughs.]

Roger was instrumental in coming up with the idea of the Zarathustra, the clap of light, the thunder on the mountain, the reincarnation, evil turns to goodness. We used the same girl. It made it a much stronger picture by having the same girl. People say, "Is that—? That's the same girl!" And that was his contribution to *Supervixens,* which was large. He did the narrative for *Up!* under the name of Rheinhold Timme. Let's see, he also did the Greek chorus on *Beneath the Valley of the Ultravixens.*

You can put an ad in Variety and say, "I want three — no — one enormously good-figured woman." You get nine hundred thousand calls from men for a part. I said, "I advertised for a woman." "I know, but we know what you're going to do. We get a lot to do." As a rule you never find anybody with an ad. The only one I ever found was Lorna Maitland.

Oh, yea! I stand corrected. *Vixen* (1968). Erica Gavin was stripping down at The Losers, which was a very good club where a lot of the girls I've worked with have worked. It was on La Cienega. Someone put the small ad in her hand and said, "Here, why don't you call?" Boy, it was just the greatest break I ever had because, Erica Gavin didn't have the best body or the biggest tits, but she had an undefinable something that made that picture work. She also appealed to women as much as to men. I don't mean in a lesbian sense, but I'm talking about her attitude towards being the user. Edy Williams, she'd want to see it once a week. See, I have a 16mm print. And she'd just come out fucking like hell that night. The whole thing just turned her on so.

About the shooting, I would say this: that it's a miracle you ever finish the picture. Each time you have to be like Simon Legree or a galley master on a Roman slave barge, indifferent to any sort of over-exertion or tiredness. The problem is that you tend to lay too much praise on a girl and she starts to . . You run out of superlatives. The men want to get laid, or they want to rush off somewhere and place their bodies on an interstate highway. All they need to do is be hit in a car and the bankroll's gone, right? It's a miracle that any of these independent films out were finished. It was only through just being hard as nails and driving everyone to the utmost, and bullshitting with all kinds of superlatives about "you'll be a star." Whatever did the job. You know, lie, cheat, steal, whatever. But always pay them, always feed them. Put a roof over their head. But don't talk to me about your biological problems. No, your husband can't come along. I consider him to be the enemy, I tell them. You know why? I can't compete with pillowtalk. And then they're going to be watching you in the sack with Pat Wright, and they're going to be mad and angry, they won't lay you and be pissed off so you don't do your job, so keep your fucking husband away. That's why we're out thirty miles in the desert. That's why I always went somewhere where hopefully there'd be nothing more than a Greyhound bus that they could catch. Because they were my captives. And they

damn well had to finish the film.

We were wondering why you prefer to use the desert.

The picture, by and large, doesn't demand extras. If it does, we use the five man crew. Everybody's been in at least one. I like the desert because it's invigorating. I love the heat, the dryness, better than anything else. I don't like to work in cold weather because the girls are uncomfortable. I love the desert.

The role of "Soul" [Uschi Digart] in Cherry, Harry & Raquel. *The film might have worked without it, but it adds so much.*

Well, without it the film would not have been complete, because the leading lady quit before we were through with her. Miss Ashton. She had been brought up to a place called Panamint, where there's not even a phone. There was a gas station and a restaurant which served terrible food. Salmon cakes every night. [Laughs.] Just an awful thing to eat.

Ashton had been a Miami showgirl. She was also the girlfriend of an important agent. Big outfit. He was with ICM or something. She didn't mind showing her ass and she had a good figure. But she insisted upon bringing two dogs up to this area. She kept them locked up in her room with the air conditioner on. Now, the guy who owned this motel was a real redneck. And the dogs would shit and piss in the room. He started complaining. He said, "You've got to let them be out, tied under a tree." She said, "Mind your own business. The dogs are going to stay in where

Stripper Virginia Bell photographed by Meyer for *Adam* magazine

45

it's cool." He said, "I'll tell you what I'm going to do. I'm going to take those dogs when you're working and tie them to a tree. They'll be in the shade and well cared for and have water." And she quit. Just quit before the film was over and went home. And there we were. We didn't have everything we thought we needed.

When Uschi showed up, I was trying to figure out how to put it together with some bridging shots. As it turned out, it was a blessing. Because Uschi was just an incredible lady. She'd do anything. She'd run over bare coals and cut glass. I mean literally! She was that kind of chick. And we became close friends. She saved the film. She made it. That's it. So that sort of thing is not as a rule done. It usually fails, if something happens, if an actor passes away or something. But I was fortunate to find a real anchor breast person. And there she was: Uschi Digard.

One of the writers on that film is listed as "Tom Wolfe."

Oh, that's my indolent partner, TJ McGowan. I knew him in the service. TJ McGowan, an interesting and amusing fellow. He got out of our outfit and he looked for something better. Then we were thrown together after the war. He tried his hand at producing plays, which he didn't do particularly well. And then he lucked onto shooting a lot of films for Disney, "The Dog Who Thought He Was a Racoon," "Sancho the Steer." They were good documentary films that Disney would pick up, and they'd play in theaters and eventually on television.

Then he wanted to do a film with me. He had some equipment, so we ponied up some money. He was kind of a co-producer/co-investor. But he didn't feel too keenly about working. He felt that I could work in the place of two men and he'd sit in the shade under an industrial-strength umbrella. Really irritated me. But he did come to me finally after he had gotten his paydays, says, "You know, I got to tell you, you put my kids through college." But I never really felt that inclined towards him again.

What became of Jack Moran, who wrote Faster Pussycat, Kill! Kill!

Jack Moran was really an important child star, Jackie Moran. If you look on the American Movie Channel and so on, you'll see he made a hundred films. He did important ones like *Since You Went Away*. He played in *Gone With the Wind*

as a little boy. He worked all the time. His father had been some sort of ward man, a politician, in Chicago. He brought the boy out to Hollywood and the tad made a lot of money. Unfortunately, at the time, this was before the Coogan law. The old man just dissipated all his dough. So Jack fell on bad times, and a friend of mine met him under less than ideal circumstances. This army buddy said, "Well, I know a guy I think can write pretty well. You ought to meet." So I did. He wrote some narration for a really dreadful film I made called *Erotica* (1961).

Shari Eubanks in *Supervixens*

[Pitchman's emphasis.] *Erotica!* It begins with two girls. One we called "Miss Glendale Salute." She couldn't use her name. She was credit manager for a Chevy agency. The other was Sheri Knight, a really impossibly buxom woman. And that was great. She came out and I met her on the beach — It was intended — and all she came in was a housecoat and a giant stole. She was pleasant as hell ... just got rolling around there on the beach. Just the damnedest thing you ever saw in your life. By golly, really something else. Hugely built. I shot a hundred feet of 16mm Kodachrome. But we didn't know what to do with it. Then got an idea to go down to a local zoo. I shot the bears ... they were rolling around and then I cut to this [laughs] giant busted woman that defied gravity, then to the bears. It was great! OK, how did I get into that? You asked me something.

We got there from Jack Moran.

Oh, all right. Moran wrote the narration for it. And then I did *Wild Gals of the Naked West* [aka *The Immoral West* (1962)]. Well into the writing Jack said, "I'd like to do the narrative." Every day he wanted to get paid. So many words, so many dollars. That was it ... brown bag lunch and a big bottle of booze. He liked to drink. So when I had written the "Pussycat" treatment, I figured I just wanted someone else to do it. Moran agreed. Same proposition. So many bucks a day, so many words. Brown bag, big bottle of hooch, cheap motel, that's all.

He started getting on the sauce pretty good. I had to bring him to my place and lock him in so he'd work for me. I said, "I'm locking you inside. I'll be here in case there's a fire, I'll break the door down, whatever. When you're finished for the night, you get your jug." And he said, "All right." He worked like a steam engine. Now he is a counselor for people who want to stop drinking. I got a letter from him a year ago, but haven't heard from him since. Insatiable smoker. One lung and he refused to stop smoking. I'm afraid to think what might have happened to him, because he was a charming guy. [Meyer has informed us that Jack Moran passed away since this interview.] He also wrote *Common-Law Cabin* (1967) and *Good Morning and Goodbye* (1967).

We had an interesting experience with *Pussycat*. We were sitting in a little cafe on Beachwood Avenue having coffee and in comes a kid with a t-shirt, *Faster Pussycat*. A bootleg. I don't care. It's alright. I said to the kid, "Where'd you get that?" He said, "Aw, I bought it somewhere." I said, "You're not going to likely believe this, but this man sitting right across from me wrote *Faster Pussycat, Kill! Kill!!*" The guy says, "Sure." He never said anything more. [Laughs.] He walked out.

Why is there so little nudity in Common-Law Cabin as compared to your other films?

Because we're in the drive-in era. You see, the passion pit era was really lucrative for me. Except when *Common-Law Cabin* came out, it signaled the end of it. They were going into complexes, ten theaters, six theaters and so forth. The drive-in theaters were bottoming out. But the ones that did well: *Mudhoney*, which didn't have a lot of nudity, and *Motorpsy-*

cho (1965), and *Faster Pussycat, Kill! Kill!*, which strangely wasn't anywhere nearly successful at the time as it became later.

In the beginning, how did your films which had nudity fare?

They played in hardtops. They played in — really— in commercial theaters when they first came out. Like for example, *Teas* played in the Fox West Coast Theater in San Diego. Opened there. They busted it after twenty minutes. After a year of being banned, finally my partner De Cenzie showed it to one of the last remaining censor boards, which was in Seattle.

(Pete [DeCenzie] was traveling with three women that he would refer to as "Pictures and Poses." He'd go out to these scumbag burlesque theaters and put on this kind of silly thing. The women would be "Dawn" or "Eve" and pose, but they couldn't move or shake their tits or anything else.)

Pete was Italian. He met another *paisan*, a censor board member. So he arranged a screening for *Mr. Teas*. The guy said, "OK, we'll look at it. I'll get the rest of the board and we'll look at it in your suite." So Pete ran out and rented a suite ... then he got a lot of Italian carry-out and dago red. And then the censor board looked at the picture. I remind you that this picture at this juncture was just "forget-it-time." You couldn't play it anywhere. It was just too damn strong. In spite of that, they passed it. Completely. Probably three sheets to the wind to boot. [Laughs.]

We went right into a theater on Fifth Avenue. It played for nearly two years.

The next big shock was when *Lorna* came out. See, there are five films I consider to be significant in my success. First, there's *Mr. Teas,* which opened up the floodgates, as it were. *Lorna* was the gritty copy of "Paisan" and "Bitter Rice" and all that ... only it was shot here in the United States and the girl's tits were bigger. So that largely made it a big success. Again, not in drive-ins. Hardtops. At first in art houses, and then it branched out into regular straight-run theaters.

Then I backed off. I said, now I'm going to make a film that doesn't have as much nudity [*Mudhoney*]. It wasn't successful until it got in the drive-ins. It was a disappointment because Lorna didn't look the same. Her tits had kinda gone south.

So that's the reason. You make them for a specific reason.

Tell us about Stuart Lancaster. He comes across so strong on screen, what's he like in person?

Stuart is a very charming friend of mine. There's a piece up here [indicates a poster on the wall] written by Hans Peter Kochenrath. He's a well-known German critic. He was talking about "Pussycat": "The films of Russ Meyer are a shameless mixture of the Hollywood cinema and an America between *Bonanza* and Vietnam. His pictures are full of disreputable Amer-

Uschi Digart in *Supervixens*

icans, man-killing women, cowardly men, greedy businessmen, and immoral farmers." He was talking about Stuart Lancaster there. [Laughs.] Immoral farmers. "All are imprisoned in a web of brutality, sex..."

Anyway, Stuart is an heir to the Ringling-North fortune. But it's doled out, so much a month. Like four thousand dollars a month, something like that. If his mother gave him all the money at once, he would have produced two hundred rotten plays. Unfortunately, he's into the theater. So, now, advance forward. He's close to me. I like him very much and he's been such a fine actor in all these pictures. But he's never had the get-up-and-go to get out there and get an agent.

Ebert was here the other night, just after the [Academy] awards. Dropped by, said, "Let's say hello to Stuart." Stuart came to the door blinking. Says, "You

know, I am seventy years of age, and today because of one of your films I was just cast in an important film being produced by Alan Alda. I've got four weeks work at four thousand a week. Who would've believed that I'd have to be seventy before I could hit the big time?

He had a kind of a good obsession for sex. I remember in *Supervixens* he played opposite Uschi Digard, who played Supersoul. He was the immoral farmer. He always had half a hard-on anyway. They were on this bed and she sat on his face, he just enjoyed her so much. He took carte blanche. [Laughs.] She was a good sport about it. Lancaster is just something else. He's just a charming guy. So what was the question?

We were just wondering about Lancaster.

He's perverse in so far as, you know, just shamelessly getting an erection under his bib overalls and [laughs] lusting for somebody. Hoping, somehow, that I would not interfere with his getting it together with somebody. Stuart, who has a terrible sense of direction, was a first lieutenant in the Navy who ferried admirals around the South Pacific. They'd send him out looking for some atoll to land with the admiral. I'd say, "How the fuck did you ever find —?" "'Cause you get a good navigator, you know."

Is there a particular film of yours that is a favorite?

No. I think, if I have my choice — there are extenuating reasons — it is *Beyond the Valley of the Dolls*. Both Ebert and I went to Fox, which had not been open to us before. We were asked to come and were given a considerable amount of money to write a script, which he did, and produce and direct it. Did exactly what we wanted to do. As he said, "They put two nuts in charge of the asylum." We did exactly what we wanted. [Studio head Dick] Zanuck had no idea about the film. He'd go and look at the rushes and come out puzzled.

But that represents having been to the mountain. My career wouldn't have been nearly as exciting if I had not been to a major studio. The reason being why I had never been asked to do it was I had to make an X-rated film. It's got to be an X, and an X is the worst thing that can happen to a major studio. It's got to be cut to an R. That's bullshit.

(continued on page 134)

the Cocktail Hour

What is a cocktail? Is it a daiquiri, a martini, a manhattan? It is all of these. But a cocktail is much more than a subtle blend of soothing ingredients. It is a promise . . . promise that the day of work is done . . . promise of the scent of exotic perfume and the sparkle of light that glistens from an earring suspended above a soft, white shoulder. The cocktail is a helpful conspirator as two pair of eyes whisper silent promises with their gaze. The cocktail symbolizes a well being of the spirit, the rustle of a silk skirt; it slips beneath the outer covering of men and women to lay bare that which is honestly theirs to share. So pause a while, friend, as the first touch of evening softens all things that by day have seemed harsh. Take the soft hand of the lady at your side and dream those dreams that are nearest to your heart. They can come true and at no other time will their fulfillment seem so near. For this is the cocktail hour. . .

YO HO HO...
AND A BOTTLE OF RUM

RUM and deeds of derring-do were once intimate. The hot, spicy fragrance and eternal goodness of rum exerted a powerful influence in pre-Revolutionary days; it fathered, so to speak, the rebellion that gave birth to this nation. Heartening swigs inspired the oratory of the day and it gave courage to the soldiers in the American Revolution. Pirates and privateers, brave men, bold and bloodthirsty, spiced their flagging spirits with dollops of rum and drove on to victory.

On the fateful night when Paul Revere thundered out of Boston on his historic ride through a star-freckled night,

destiny rode with him. On the route was the home and the rum distillery of Isaac Hall, and Revere stopped for one for the road with his friend. They probably quaffed a long and hearty toast to the confusion of the British.

Rum raised a lively and lovely head all through the conflict that followed; it was the medicine of the wounded, the solace of both Tory and patriot. Today, too, it is comforting solace and one of the favored beverages of the populace in mixed drinks during the dog days of Summer heat. As of yore, rum is the stable ingredient of hundreds of the tastiest frosty delights, perhaps the best

Spicy aromatic goodness of rum helped write U. S. history
and is still savored today for its charm and suave sophistication
in a multitude of wonderfully-tasting summer drinks.

By Harry Botsford

combination of ice and alcohol ever discovered. Imaginative bar-tenders never cease experimentation with new rum drinks and are continually inventing new concoctions.

Rare today is the man who drinks rum straight, yet at one time that was the main way Americans quaffed the stuff. Those were the pre-1776 days.

The British knew a good thing, and they were willing to fight for it: they wanted to keep the Colonies under their dominion and they wanted to force the colonists to pay a stiff tax on their favorite tipple. They were willing to pay a price of blood and lives to accomplish this fell pur-

pose. A group of loosely-knit colonies, our population was estimated at 2,500,000 Americans who consumed about 12,000,000 gallons of rum annually.

The war was largely fought on salt pork, jerked venison, journey cake and rum. Some of the rum was distilled locally; much of it came to the shores we controlled by daring smugglers who played tag with the cumbersome, slow-moving British armed ships.

Rum was a prime necessity. John Hancock, no man to bandy words, once wrote heatedly, "As to rum, it is of such importance that the army should be fill'd up and regularly supplied," a statement that was echoed by every patriot bearing arms.

No other tipple pleased the fancy of the pioneers as much as rum. It was the drink most often called for in the taverns; it was equally at home on the hospitable sideboards of gracious mansions and in obscure log cabins. The clergy gave it their blessing, the physicians of the day prescribed it for patients who suffered from everything from colic to cancer. Births were celebrated with rum, it flowed at christenings, and there was a deluge to solace the mourners at a funeral. It was the tavern of the village that was the real temple of rum. It was in good supply, it had economy, and the tavern was the place where people gathered to drink, swap ideas, trade, surreptitiously talk treasonably about a thing called independence and liberty. The village tavern was established by law as a colonial convenience for travelers and a village that did not have one, could expect to be fined.

In the taverns, the most popular drink was a Flip, Bounce, Sling, Shrub, Sour Julep and Punch. Each served a special purpose, depending on the mood of the consumer. A tavern owner in Pennsylvania, a gentleman with a nice sense of the eternal fitness of things, a citizen blessed with a daring turn of mind, the spirit of gallantry that lies behind experimental research, came up with a rum drink that leaped into instant popularity. Later versions were to be dubbed "Tom and Jerry."

The recipe was somewhat involved. Served in a wooden or pewter tankard, it was a certain panacea against the rigors of cold weather, a toddy of sorts. About it, one rural logician neatly stated: "It is both food and drink—and if you have enough, it is also lodging for the night."

As compounded by the deft hands of the Pennsylvania tavern keeper, the recipe called for one fresh egg, a good portion of dry West Indies rum, one small spoon of sugar, one-quarter that amount of all-spice, and of good brandy about one quarter of the volume of the rum. Into this went the yolk of the egg. The egg white was beaten separately to a stiff froth. The tankard was rinsed in boiling water, the contents dumped in it and the tankard was filled with boiling water, the top covered with a dapple of nutmeg. Unhappily, the precise quantities of the spirits required for this steaming brew are not known, but I will warrant you it was ample.

Let the blizzard howl, let the snow and frost etch patterns on the windows, but there would be a roaring log fire in the fireplace, the mellow light of candles would light the interior. There would be the hum of good talk; the crowd would be democratic; the tankards would be raised often by red-faced men who stood with their backs to the fire. The travelers would relate the latest news; the men would talk about crops and the harvest of furs, the arrivals of ships, the price of powder, the sweetness of the wicked and lovely women they had known and bedded with. Voices would drop, someone would speak of the tyranny of England, the Liberty Tree Boys, men who were soon destined to greatness and fame. Rum made the Winter

nights pleasant. A red-hot loggerhead would hiss as it was plunged into a tankard of what was called "One Yard of Flannel," and the air was permeated with the delightful, spicy fragrance of rum.

"One Yard of Flannel" was compounded of a pint of cream, four beaten eggs, 1 cup of brown sugar, one-half spoon of ground ginger and nutmeg. A quart pewter mug was filled two-thirds full of hard cider, four great spoons of the mixture were added with a gill of rum, the contents were stirred, and the red hot loggerhead was thrust in it. The aroma was such that it stimulated the appetites of the traveling guests, and they peered anxiously at the spits turning before the fire. On the spits would be a haunch of venison, a lordly roast of beef, a dozen fowls attaining maturity, basted with the pan juices to which a modicum of rum had been added. In the ovens, journey cake was baking.

Ease and comfort, that's the picture painted of an evening spent in a tavern, and the colors are vivid and memorable, pleasant and engaging.

The rum of those days was undoubtedly stronger than what is available today. It lacked the purity, the clarity, the uniformity that characterizes modern rums. It was, as a rule, rum from the West Indies, which did not please the British overmuch. The truth was Spain had outsmarted England on the volume and the quality of rum it produced. They put the raw rum in great tuns, packed fresh horse manure around it to heat and purify the lethal contents, further purified by running it through beds of sand.

As early as 1511, Spain produced the most and the best of rums. They owned Hispaniola (now Haiti), Puerto Rico, Cuba and Jamaica. The climate was ideal for raising sugar cane. They had an abundance of slaves and when they needed more, they traded raw rum for recruits. They had mills to crush the cane, the refineries to make the molasses from which rum is produced, and cool, clean mountain water. They were 132 years ahead of the British.

Their rums were superior, light and heady, spicy as to aroma. They could form the base of a light, convivial tipple, or they could be used to form a drink with the potency and velocity of a West Indian hurricane.

Their ships were fast, their men were good and crafty sailors. During many of the years a state of open warfare existed between France and England, their ships were agile and they made an art of smuggling their rum-laden ships in the ports of the colonies, with special attention paid to the Southern colonies.

Of the original four island sources of rum, England today controls only one: Jamaica. Cuba and Haiti are independent nations while Puerto Rico is an integral part of the United States. Of all the rums consumed in the United States, the little island produces about two-thirds of what we drink.

If the impression has been given that the taverns served only steaming hot rum drinks, may your scribe hasten to say that rum was a year-around

(continued on page 138)

SCOTCHED

Inspiring bold John Barleycorn!
What dangers thou canst make us scorn!
Wi' tippeny, we face nae evil:
Wi' usquabae, we'll face the devil!

Tam o'Shanter, Robert Burns, 1791

Sir Lyn MacHayashi

I canna remember all the beauties at hoisted up my kilt, but I ken (now) the scotch that stained my lips rever.

Whisky and whiskey be two fferent spellings. "Whisky" be from :otland, Japan and Canada. "Whiskey" e from America, Ireland and elsewhere. And most importantly, if a whisky is to be called scotch, it must be both distilled and matured in Scotland.

Malting, mashing, fermentation, distillation and maturation produce the water of life. Malting is the steeping of barley in water to encorage germination. The green malt is then dried over peat burning furnaces. Mashing grinds the dried malt into a course flour which is mixed with hot water and yeast to start the fermentation process. Distillation vaporized the spirit which then condenses and collected in vats. The maturation is a most mysterious process. The new spirit is clear. Oak casks that previously held sherry are widely used to impart the amber color as it matures. Some distilleries add a wee bit of carmel coloring. By law, scotch whisky must be aged for a least three years. There is much opinion regarding the optimum age for scotch, the common ages being eight, 10, 12, 15, 18, 21 and upwards.

There are four types of scotch. The standard blends that mix as many as 50 individual malt and grain whiskies, are Ballantines's, Cutty Sark, Dewar's, J&B and Johnnie Walker Red Label. The de luxe blends that contain a higher proportion of older whiskies are Chivas Regal, Johnnie Walker Black Label and Usquaebach. The forerunner of both standard and de luxe blends is vatted scotches which combine different malts only. Vatted scotches are a rare breed and the best known are Mar Lodge, Pride of Strathspey and Strathconon.

By the grace o'god, there are single malt scotches, the product of a single distillery. The American scotch market is 97% blended drinkers and only 3% drinking single malt scotches such as Blair Athol, Bruichladdich, Cardhu, Dallas Dhu, Glenfiddich, Glenlivet, Glenmorangie, Highland Park, Isle of Jura, Knockando, Lagavulin, Macallan, Oban, Rosebank, Sheep Dip and Talisker.

I am breathing in Springbank, a 21-year-old single malt from Campbeltown. It tastes of sea mist in Kintyre with a round, profound character. Springbank prides itself on not chill-filtering its product nor adding carmel coloring. It was during the American

(continued page 139)

WASSAIL!

Gone are the days when a fellow might step into a bar or buffet and overhear, at a nearby table, an eloquent toast followed by the convivial clink of glasses. Toasting used to be an important process of social communion and a hearty enhancement of the dining experience. Now it is neither. Why have we wandered from this charming and civilized tradition?

In his book, *Toasts,* author Paul Dickson tells us that "it is impossible to point to the moment when the first rude vessel was raised in honor of an ancient god or to the health of a newborn baby," but he does cite the early example of Ulysses' drinking to Achilles in the *Odyssey.* He suggests that over the course of time toasting became more elaborate. The tradition of clinking the glasses was originally meant to "produce a bell-like noise so as to banish the devil."

The Cad's Guide To Creative Toasting

Come hither, my lads with your tankards of ale,
And drink to the present before it shall fail;
Pile each on your platter a mountain of beef,
For 'tis eating and drinking that brings us relief:
So fill up your glass,
For life will soon pass;
When you're dead ye'll ne'er drink to your king or
    your lass!
— H. P. Lovecraft

Come goblet — nymph of lovely shape,
Pour the rich weepings of the grape

Fill me, lad, as deep a draught
As e'er was filled, as e'er was quaff'd.
Grasp the bowl, in nectar sinking,
Man of sorrow, drown thy thinking!

Here's to the girl I love,
I wish that she were nigh;
If drinking beer would bring her here,
I'd drink the damn place dry

Champagne to your real friends,
And real pain to your sham friends

Fill, fill, fill the brimming glass,
Each man toasts his favorite lass,
He who flinches is an ass,
Unworthy of love or wine

Here's to woman,
The only sewing machine that ever basted a goose

A mocking eye,
A pair of lips,
That's often why
A fellow trips

Here's to the girl who lives on the hill
She won't but her sister will
So here's to her sister

To your genitalia
May they never jail ya'

May the devil make a ladder of your backbone
While he is picking apples in the garden of hell

May you all be Hung, Drawn and Quartered!
Yes — hung with diamonds,
Drawn in a coach and four
And quartered in the best houses in the land

Here's to a long life and a merry one,
A quick death and an easy one,
A pretty girl and a true one,
A cold bottle and another one

about done
about full
about gone
about had it
about right
about shot
a-buzz
account, casting
  up his
aced
activated
addled
adrip
afflicted
afloat
aglow
alcoholized
alecie
ale-washed
alight
alkied
alkied up
alky soaked
all at sea
all geezed up
all gone
all in
all liquored-up
all lit-up
all mops and brooms
all out
all sails spread
all schnozzled
all there
all wet
almost frozen
altogethery
anchored in sot's bay
angel-altogether
antifreezed
antiseptic
aped
ape drunk
asotus
ass on backwards
at ease
at rest
awash
awry-eyed
Bacchus-bulged
Bacchus-butted
back home
bagged
baked
balmy
bamboozled
bang through
  the elephant
baptized
bar, over the
barleysick
barmy
barreled (up)
barrel fever
barrelhouse drunk
bashed
basted
batted
battered
batty
bay, over the
bears, see the
been among the
  Phillipians
been among the
  Philistines
been at an
  Indian feast
been at Barbados
been at Geneva
been in a storm
been in the
  bibbing plot
been in the
  crown office

been in the sauce
been in the sun
been to a funeral
been to France
been to Jericho
been to Olympus
been to the saltwater
been to free
  with Sir John
been too free with
  the creature
  strawberry
been with
  Sir John Goa
beerified
beer soaked
befuddled
beginning to fly
behind the cork
belly up
belted
bending over
bent
bent an elbow
bent and broken
bent out of shape
besot
bewildered
bewottled
beyond salvage
bezzled
bibacious
bibulous
biled owl
biffy
biggy
bingoe
bit
bit by a fox
bit his grannan
bit his name in
bit on
bit teed
bit tiddley
bit tipsy
bit wobbly
bite in the brute
bitten by a
  barn mouse
blanked
blasted
blighted
blimped
blind
blind drunk
blinded
blink, on the
blinking drunk
blinky
blissed
blistered
blithered
blitzed
bloated
block and block
blowed
blown
blown away
blown over
blown up
blowzy blue
blue around the gills
blue eyed
blued
boggled
bowzered
boxed
brained
brass eye, have a
breaky leg
breezy
brewer's basket, stole
  a manchet out of a
brick in his hat,
  got a

bridgey
bright eyed
brook, pissed in the
bruised
bubbed
bubbled
buckled
budgey
buffy
bug-eyed
bulge
bummed
bumpsie
bumpsy
bun
bun on, have a
bung-eyed
bunged
bungy
bunned
buoyant
burdocked
buried
burn with a low
  (blue) flame
burried
burst
business on both
  sides of the way
busky
busted
buzzed
buzzey
buzzy
cached
caged
came home by the
  villages
canned (up)
canon
can't hit the ground
  with his hat
can't see through
  a ladder
can't sport a
  right light
can't walk a chalk
cap sick
capable
capers, cuts his
cargoed
carrying a heavy load
carrying a load
carrying two
  red lights
cast
cat
catched
catsood
caught
cellar, he's in the
chagrined
chapfallen
charged
cheary
cherubimical
chickery
chipper
chirping merry
chocked
chucked
clear out
clinched
coagulated
coarse
cocked
cocked as a log
cocked to the gills
cockeyed
coguy
colored
comboozelated
comboozled
commin' (on)
completely gone

completely out of it
completely squashed
concerned
Concord, half way to
conflummoxed
corned
cornered
coxy-foxy
cracked
crackling
cramped
crapulous
crashed
crazed
crazy
creamed
crocked
crocko
crocus
cronk
crooked
cropsick
crosseyed
crowning office,
  in the
crump
crump fooled
crumped (out)
crying jag
cuckooed
cup too much
cupped

cups, in his
cupshot
curved
cushed
cut
cut in the craw
D and D
daffy
dagged
damaged
damp
dark day with him
dead to the world
decayed
deck(s) awash
deep cut
deep drunk
defaced
demoralized
derailed
detained on business
devil, seen the
dew drunk
dewed
diddled
ding swizzled
dinged
dingy
dinky
dipped
dipsy
dirtfaced
discombobulated
discomboobulated

discouraged
discumfuddled
disguised
dished
dish, got a
disorderly
distinguished
dithered
dizzy
do a Daniel Boone
do an edge
dog, killed his
done a Falstaff
done an Archie
done over
done up
doped
doped over
dotted
dotty
double-headed
double-tongued
doubled-up
down and out
down for the count
down with the fish
drunk in his dumpes
drunkok
drunkulent
drunky
due for drydock
dull-eyed
dumped

ears are ringing
ebrios
ebrious
edge
edged
edge on, have an
electrified
elephant's trunk
elevated
eliminated
embalmed
entered
exalt
exalted
example, made an
exhilarated
extinguished
faced
feel aces
feel dizzy
feel frisky
feel glorious
feel good
feel happy
feel his booze
feel his liquor
feel juiced-up
feel the effect
feeling no pain
fettered
feverish
fiddle-cup
fiddled
fired-up

fishey
fish-eyed
fishy
fishy about the gills
fishy-eyed
fixed
fizzed
fizzled
flag is out
flaked out
flakers
flako
flared
flat out drunk
flatch-kennurd
flawed
floating
flood one's sewers
flooded
flooey
floopy
floored
florid
florious
flostered
fluffy
flummixed
flush
flushed
fluster
flusterate
flusterated
flustered
flusticate
flusticated

fly-blown
fly high
flying blind
flying high
flying light
flying on one wing
flying the ensign
fogged
foggy
fogmatic
folded
foolish
forward
fossilized
four sheets in
  (to) the wind
fox, caught a
fox-drunk
foxy
fractured
frazzled
free and easy
fried
fried on both sides
friend, spoke with his
froze his mouth
frozen
fucked over
fuddle one's cap
fuddle one's nose
fuddled
fuddled as an ape
full
full as a boot

full as a bull
full as a fiddler
full as a goat
full as a goose
full as a lord
full as a tick
full as an egg
full of hops
full cargo
full-cocked
full-flavored
full of courage
full to the bung
full up
funny feeling
fully soused
fully tanked
fur-brained
fur on his tongue
fuzzled
fuzzy
fuzzy-headed
gaffed
gaga
gage
gaged, boozed the
galvanized
gargled
gaseous
gassed
gassy
gay
gayed
geared-up
geed
geeded
geed-up
geesed
generous
Geneva, been at
George, been before
get a bun on
get a glow on
get a jag on
get a load on
get a shithouse on
get a skate on
get a snootful
get a thrill
get an edge on
get barreled up
get bleary-eyed
get blotto
get boozed-up
get bung-eyed
get boozy
get canon
get charged-up
get crocked
get cut
get dopy
get flushed
get full
get glorious
get goofy
get high
get jungled
get light-headed
get likkered-up
get lit
get loaded
get looped
get loose
get organized
get pickled
get right
get shot
get sloppy
get soused
get stiff
get tanked-up
get the big head
get the gage up
get there with
  both feet

get topsy
get warmed
get wasted
get wet
get whizzy
get woozy
giddy
gizzled
gild
gilded
gill, blue around t
gills, filled to the
gills, green
  around the
gills, loaded to the
gin-crazed
gingered
ginned
ginny
glad
glaized
glanders
glassy, got the
glassy-eyed
glazed
globular
glorious
glowed
glowing
glow on
glued
god-awful drunk
good and drunk
gowed to the gills
had a couple
  of drinks
had a dram
had a few too man
had a little
had a little too ma
had a snort
had his cold tea
had one or two
hair on his tongue
haily gaily
half-canned
half-cocked
half-corked
half-corned
half-crocked
half-cut
half-geared
half-gone
half-goofed
half in the bag
half in the boot
half-jacked
half-lit
half-loaded
half-looped
half-mocus
half-muled
half-on
half-out
half-pickled
half-pissed
half-rats
half-rinsed
half-screwed
half-seas over
half-shaved
half-shot
half-slewed
half-snaped
half-sober
half-soused
half-sprung
half-stewed
half-stiff
half-tanked
half the bay over
half the bay under
half-tipsy
half-under
half up the pole

THE DRUNKARD'S THESAURUS

'way to Concord
ımered
ımerish
ıced
py
a bag on
a brass eye
a brick
one's hat
a bun on
a can on
a drop in his eye
a full cargo
a glow on
a guest
the attic
a jag on
a load on
a package on
a shine on
a skate on
a slant on
a snoot full
an edge on
business on
the screaming
ʒemies
the whoops
d jingles
the zings
got on his little
ınted with evil
rits
y
d, got by the
ring the owl hoot
ʒed
s a little
ʒup
ius-doccius
us
ʒey
ʒley

as a fiddler
as a
orgia pine
as a kite
as Lindbergh
as the sky
lonesome
up to
ʒking cotton
ʒer than a kite
ʒed
ʒy a barnmouse
ʒy-eyed
ʒky
ʒkey
us pocus
drunk
ʒked
ʒched
ʒch up
ʒdman
ʒted
ʒped
ʒped-up
ʒup
zontal
ʒnson
ʒeback, got the
ʒd
ʒheaded
ʒer than a skunk
ʒcome-ye-so
ʒinated
ʒbed too much
fix
fog
fuddle
muddle
stew
trance

in armor
in beer
in color
in drink
in for it
in his airs
in his ales
in his altitudes
in his armor
in his beer
in his glory
in his pots
in his prosperity
in liquor
in orbit
in the bag
in the cellar
in the clouds
in the gutter
in the pen
in the pink
in the pulpit
in the rats
in the sack
in the satchel
in the suds
in the sun
in the tank
in the wind
in uncharted waters
incognito
indisposed
inebriate
inebriated
infirm
influenced
inked
inspired
into the suds
inundated
irrigated
jag up
jagged
jagged-up
jambled
jammed
jarred
jazzed
jazzed-up
Jerusalem, going to
jiggered
jingled
jocular
jolly
jug-bitten
jug-steamed
jugged
juiced
juiced-up
juicy
jungled
kennurd
Kentucky fried
kettle, chase the
kettle, hit his
keyed
keyed-up
keyed to the roof
kib'd heels
kicked in the guts
killed
killed one's dog
king, he's a
king is his cousin
king, seen the French
kisky
kissed the
   Black Betty
kited
knapt
knee-crawling drunk
knee-walking drunk
knocked for a loop
knocked off his pins
knocked out

knocked over
knocked up
knockered
knows the way home
laced
laid out
laid right out
laid to the bone
lame
lap in the gutter
lappy
lathered
leaning
leaping
leaping up
leary
leery
leggs, makes
   indentures with his
legless
leveled
lifted
light
light-headed
likkered
likkered-up
likkerous
limber
limp
lined
lion drunk
liquified
liquor, in
liquor struck
liquor up
liquored
liquored-up
liquorish
listing
lit
lit a bit
lit to the gills
lit to the guards
lit to the gunnels
lit up
lit up like a cathedral
lit up like a
   Christmas tree
lit up like a church
lit up like a
   high mass
lit up like a kite
lit up like
   a skyscraper
lit up like a
   store window
lit up like Broadway
lit up like
   Main Street
lit up like
   Times Square
lit up like the
   Catholic Church
lit up like the sky
little tight
little woozy
live well, to
load one's card
loaded
loaded for bear
loaded his cart
loaded to the barrel
loaded to the
   earlobes
loaded to the gills
loaded to the guards
loaded to the gunnels
loaded to the
   gunwales
loaded to the hat
loaded to the muzzle
loaded to the
   plimsoll mark
lock-legged
logged

look blue about
   the gills
loony
loop-legged
looped
looped-legged
loopy
loose in the hilt
loppy
lord, drunk as a
lordly
lost his rudder
lousy drunk
love-dovey
lubricated
lumped
lumpy
lushed
lushed-up
lushy
mainbrace is
   well-spliced
making scallops
malt is above wheat
   with him
malted
malty
Martin drunk
maudlin
mauled
melted
merry as a grigg
merry pin, on a
methodistconated
middling
milled
mizzled
mocus
moist around
   the edges
monuments,
   raised his
mooney
moon-eyed
mops and brooms
muddled
muddy
mugg blotts
mugged
muggy
mulled
mulled-up
murky
muzzy
nail, off the
nappy
nase
nazie
nazy
nimptopsical
nimtopsical
night mare, got the
nipped
niptopsical
noddy-headed
non compos
noppy
nose is dirty
not all there
not suffering
numb
nuts
nutty
obfuscated
obfusticated
oddish
oenomania
oenophilist
off at the nail
off his bean
off his feet
off the deep end
off to the races
oiled
on his ass

on his ear
on his fourth
on his last legs
on his way out
on the blink
on the floor
on the lee lurch
on the shikker
one-over-eight
one too many
onion, smelt of an
organized
orie-eyed
oscillated
ossified
out
out like a lamp
out like a light
out of his element
out of his mind
out of it
out of one's mind
out of the picture
out of the way
out on the roof
out to lunch
over the bay
over the mark
overboard
overcome
overdone
overloaded
overseas
overseen
overserved
overset
overshot
overtaken
overwined
owl, drunk as an
owl-eyed
owled
oxycrocium
package
package on, have a
packaged
palatic
palled
paralysed
parboiled
past gone
pasted
paunch, wasted his
peckish
pee-eyed
peekish
peonied
pepped
pepst
perked
petrificated
petrified
pickled
pigeon-eyed
pie-eyed
pied
piffed
pifficated
piffled
pigeon-eyed
pilfered
pin drunk
pinked
pinko
pious
piped
pipped
pissed
pixilated
plain drunk
plastered
plated
played out
pleasantly jingled
plonked

plotzed
ploughed
ploughed under
ploxed
pogie
pogy
poggled
pole, up the
polished
polite
polluted
pop-eyed
pot-hardy
pot shaken
pots, among the
pots, in the
pots on
potshot
potsick
potsville
potted
potty
potulent
powder up
powdered
preserved
prestoned
pretty drunk
pretty far gone
pretty happy
pretty high
pretty well plowed
pretty well
   primed priddy
primed to the barrel
primed to the muzzle
primed to the trigger
prosperity, in his
pruned
puggy
punch aboard
pungy
puppy, good-
   conditioned as a
put to bed
   with a shovel
putrid
pye-eyed
quarrelsome
queer
queered
quilted
racked
racked-up
raddled
ragged
raised
rammaged
rampage
rat in trouble
rattled
ratty
raunchy
razzle dazzled
ready
really gassed
really got a load
really lit up
really soused
really tied one on
reeking
reeling
reely
ree-raw
relaxed
religious
rest, at
revved up
rich
rigid
rileyed
ripe
ripped
roasted
rocky

rolling drunk
roostered
rorty
rosined
rosy
rotten
royal rudder, lost his
rum dumb
rummed
rummied
rummed rye
salted
salted down
salubrious
sap happy
sapped
sappy
saturated
sauced
sawed
scammered
schicker
schizzed out
schlitzed
schlockered
schnockered
schnoggered
scoop
scooped
scorched
scrambled
scratched
scraunched
screaming
screaming drunk
screetching
screwed
screwy
scronched
scrooched
scrooped
seafaring
seasick
second hand drunk
seeing a flock
   of moons
seeing bats
seeing bears
seeing double
seeing elephants
seeing the devil
seeing two moons
sell one's senses
sent
served
served-up
set up
sewed
sewed-up
shagged
shagg
shaved
shellacked

shews his hobnails
shick
shicked
shickered
shikker
shikkered
shipwrecked
shitfaced
shitty
shoe pinches him
shorty
shot
shot full of holes
shot in the head
shot in the mouth
shot in the neck
shot in the wrist
shot up
shoulder, burnt his
showing his booze
showing his drinks
showing it
silly
silly drunk
sizzled
skated
skinful
skunk drunk
skunked
skunky
slanted
slathered
sleeve-button
slewed
slewy
slick
slippery
slipping
slobbered
slopped
sloppy
sloshed
sloud
sloughed
slued
slugged
slushed
smashed
smeared
smells of the cork
smitten by the grape
smoked
snackered
snapped snockered
snooted
snootful
snootful, had a
snotted
snozzled
snubbed
snuffy
snug
soaked

soaked his face	sponge-eyed	stinking	swigged	Tipiun Grove	tuned	waxed	whittled
soaked to the gills	sponge-headed	stinking drunk	swiggled	tipped	tuned up	way, out of the	whooshed
soaken	spotty	stinko	swilled	tipping	twisted	weak-jointed	whoozy
soapey-eyed	spreed	stitched	swilled up	tippled	two sheets	weary	wilted
sobbed	spreeish	stocked up	swine drunk	tippling	to the wind	weaving	wine-potted
socked	sprinkled	stoked	swined	tipsification	ugly	well away	wine shits
sodden	sprung	stolled	swinnied	tipsified	uncorked	well-bottled	wined up
soft	squamed	stone blind	swiped	tipsy	under	well-fixed	winey
soggy	squared	stone cold drunk	swipy	tip-top	under full sail	well-heeled	wing heavy
sold his senses	squashed	stoned	switched	tired	under full steam	well-jointed	winterized
Solomon, as wise as	squiffed	stoned out	swiveled	toasted	under the table	well-lathered	wiped
sopped	squiffy	of his mind	swizzled	tongue-tied	under the weather	well-lit	wiped-out
sopping	squirrelly	stonkered	swozzled	too far north	underway	well-lubricated	wired
soppy	squished	stozzled	tacked	top-heavy	unsober	well-mulled	wise
sore-footed	staggerish	striped	tangle-footed	top-loaded	up a tree	well-oiled	wobbly
soshed	staggers	stubbed	tangled	toped	up on blocks	well-organized	woggled
sotted	stale drunk	stuccoed	tangled-legged	topped	up the pole	well-primed	woofled
sotto	starched	stung	tanked	toppled	up to the gills	well-soaked	wooshed
soused	starchy	stunked	tanked up	topp	upholster	well-sprung	woozy
soused to the ears	stark drunk	stunned	tanned	topsy turvy	upholstered	wet	wrecked
soused to the gills	steady	stupefied	tap-shacklen	torn up	uppish	wet-handed	yaupish
southern fried	steamed	stupid	taplash wretched	torrid-tossed	upsed	wettish	zagged
sow drunk	steeped	sucked	tapped	tosticated	valient	whacked out	zapped
sozzled	stewed	suds, a little in the	tapped out	totalled	varnished	what-nosed	zin zagged
sozzly	stewed to the ears	suds, in the	tapped the admiral	touched	vinolence	whazooed	zin zan
sparred	stewed to the gills	sun, been in the	tattooed	touched off	vulcanized	whiffled	zippen
speared	sticked	sun in the eyes	tean	toxed	wall-eyed	whipcan	zissified
speechless	stiff	sun over the	teeth under	toxicated	wallpapered	whipped	zoned
spiffed	stiff as a carp	fore-yard	tied one on	trammeled	wassailed	whipsed	zonked
spiffled	stiff as a goat	super-charged	tight as a	trance, in a	wassailed out	whiskeyfied	zorked
spiflicated	stiff as a plank	swacked	ten-day drunk	translated	wassailed up	whiskey-frisky	zozzled
splashed	stiff as a ramrod	swamped	tilted	trashed	wasted	whiskey-raddled	
spliced	stiff as a ring-bolt	swatched	tin hats	tripping drunk	water cart, on the	whiskey shot	
spliffcated	stiffed	swatted	tinned	tuben	water-logged	whiskey sodden	
spliffo	stimulated	swattled	tip merry	tumbled down	water-soaked	whiskied	
sploshed	stinkarooed	swazzled	tin top tippled	the sink	watered	whistle drunk	

The Driest Martini

by Frederick A. Birmingham

Can a Martini be improved upon? [O]ur answer is an emphatic no. The very [th]ought of an attempt on the part of [ma]nkind to devise anything crisper and [ref]reshinger seems so tragically futile, it [bri]ngs tears to our eyes. To be worthy of [th]e name, a Martini must be made of the [ve]ry finest vermouth and positively [su]blime gin; otherwise it is a sell and a [sw]indle and incompetent to set the mood [for] a meal.

Fortunately, the Martini vigilantes [ar]e ever on the increase, making aroma [ho]liday a frequent occurrence. And some [of] the brethren, armed with tape [me]asures and sounding sticks, are [in]vestigating the size of glasses in the [co]nviction that this drink has deeper [po]ssibilities than stingy servers realize. [Th]ey want to meet Olive when the tide's [not] wade to her.

There will never be an end, of [co]urse, to the great discourse on the [M]artini. The late Bernard DeVoto writes:

"Sound practice begins with ice. There must be a lot of it, much more than the catechumen dreams, so much that the gin smokes when you pour it in. A friend of mine has said it for all time; his formula ends "and five hundred pounds of ice." Fill the pitcher with ice, whirl it till dew forms on the glass, pour out the melt, put in another handful of ice. Then as swiftly as possible pour in the gin and vermouth, at once bring the mixture as close to the freezing point of alcohol as can be reached outside the laboratory, and pour out the martinis. You must be unhurried but you must work fast, for a diluted martini would be a contradiction in terms, a violation of nature's order. That is why the art requires so much ice and why the artist will never mix a single round at a time, counting noses."

As to the proportions of gin and vermouth, pray, gentlemen, leave us not argue. We have known men who like it,

Italian style, with plenty of vermouth to yellow the drink. We have known those who scorn the olive for the twist of lemon peel (the peel is never dropped into the drink, but squeezed in gentle proximity to it, the lover's breath on the face of the adored). We have known a man to pour vermouth on the ice, then drain it, and pour his gin over that fragrant ice. We have heard that Winston Churchill measures his vermouth by glancing at the bottle (but never touching it) while pouring the gin.

We leave the battle to you and yours. We say: gin on the rocks is not a Martini — four to one is an accepted ratio. If you would soar higher, blessings on you. And may wings waft you on your pleasant way. For gin was surely born out of beauty — Venus, perhaps — and sired by Jupiter in a flash of soft lightning.

59

The Grassy Tongue Hangover

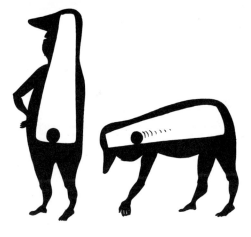

The I'm-All-Right-as-Long-as-I-Don't-Bend-Over Hangover

The Nine-Iron Hangover

The Don't-You-Hear-It-Too? Hangover

VIP

does HANGOVERS...

The Sawing-Woman-in-Half Hangover

The Ground-Zero Hangover

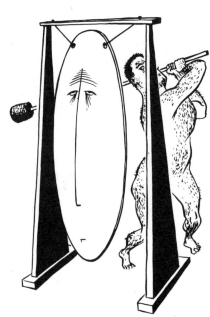

The Chicken-Little Hangover

The Rosy-Outlook Hangover

60

The Pull-Those-Goddam-Blinds Hangover

The I-Must-Have-Gone-Ten-Fast-Rounds Hangover

The Please-No-Sudden-Noises Hangover

The Whole-Ghastly-Room-Is-Spinning Hangover

The How-Can-I-Ever-Face-Them Hangover

The I-Refuse-to-Remember Hangover

The Laughing-on-the-Outside-Crying-on-the-Inside Hangover

The Nothing-Seems-Real Hangover

The Shakes Hangover

61

Phaedre Zoomboom contemplates an evening alone in her Greenwich Village flat.

HOWL BABY HOWL

Phaedre: Laura Richmond

Photographer: Scott Lindgren

Will it be groovy or will it be dullsville?

Setting the mood...

Huffing the muggles...

Spinning the Miles...

Guzzlin' the Chianti...

Goofin' on a C note...

And Move!

Like, Wow!

Needs more blue ...

... Right there ...

65

Kitten on the keys ...

Pussy times two
equals a
purr-fect end
to a swingin'
affair!

THE TRUMPET AND THE SPIKE

A CONFESSION BY CHET BAKER

The famous jazzman tells one of the most candid stories about being hooked that you are ever likely to read in your life.

I was born in Yale, Oklahoma, 34 years ago. My father was a musician, a poor, unsuccessful one, always out of a job. He could play several instruments and he wasn't bad, but he just couldn't make the grade and was nearly always around the house out of work. Naturally, we weren't exactly rich. In fact, most of the time, there was never any bread in the house at all. By bread, I mean dough, that is money, as we hips call it, but it would be true of the real bread too,

for often we didn't know where the next meager meal was coming from. Until I left home at 16, I spent my childhood and adolescence in dire poverty. My old man did go out and get other jobs, but he was a failure at each one. He didn't mind admitting it, I mean the jobs, but not the music. He would never admit he was a failure as a musician and always blamed the 1929 depression; this may have been the truth, because I understand it certainly resulted in a lot of bands shutting down and a lot of cats sitting at home.

Well, my old man was a pot-head. I discovered this quite by chance when I was only seven. One day I was up late in bed, mother was out somewhere, and the old man was in the parlor with some of his cronies. I could hear their voices as they talked, but after a while there was silence. I got out of bed, it was a sort of intuition. I crept downstaris and took a peek through the keyhole. My old man and his pals were lying back in their chairs with their eyes closed. They've gone to sleep, I thought, and they're dreaming strange, wonderful dreams. The room was filled with white smoke and its pungent smell reached me through the door and made me feel sick. I never told a soul about what I had seen, least of all my parents, and it was my old man himself who, years later when I was 14 or 15 and already playing the horn, brought up the matter.

I was quite indifferent to what he said, his confession about being a pot-head, and at the same time I had no desire to try the stuff. But God knows what the old man would have said had he been alive today and seen what had happened to his son. Pot? I've smoked thousands of cigarettes, but I've moved on to paradises and hells, which my old man for financial as much as psychological reasons had never known and could hardly imagine. But to return to myself, at 13 I bought myself a horn and taught myself to play it with the help of the old man, and at 16 I stuck it under my arm and walked out of the house.

What could I do? I had no special training and not much schooling either. It was quite by accident that I saw one of the usual recruiting posters with the slogan "Join the Army and see the World." I joined. If the poster had been a Navy one, I would have joined the Navy. Most of the world I saw was Germany. I was sent there after a short training period at home and I spent the next two years there. My horn was to prove useful after all. I managed to get into an army band. By practicing with real musicians, I improved. I played at G.I. gigs all over the country and my music gradually became my only interest in life with the result that when I left the army, at 19, I decided to become a professional jazz musician.

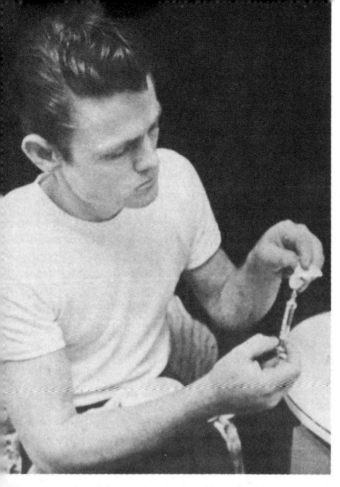

Soon I was playing in various bands and meeting a lot of cats. They accepted me and I knew I was one of them and then I met Charlie Parker ... ah, Charlie and his saxophone. We met by accident one day and he took a liking to me and asked me to play with him. I owe him everything because after being with him I never looked back again. Shortly afterwards I joined up with Gerry Mulligan and his pianoless quartet and became a top musician. Charlie was a junkie. Most musicians are, you know. But at the time I was only a pot-head.

What happens with pot is this, you smoke away regularly and sooner or later you find that its effect is going tamer and tamer. One day a friend was with me — I remember how it started well enough — and he said I should kick pot which was kids' stuff. He took a spike and showed me how to use it and suddenly I was hooked. I became a junkie. Spiking myself became a gesture as automatic as lighting a cigarette is with you. I did it thousands of times, squeezing the vein out and plunging the syringe. My veins became hardened and my arms became covered with sores — but I didn't care. A junkie never does. From

then on I was on heroin and this is where things started to get hot for me, because in New York you can get as much pot as you like — it's as simple as stopping in the street and whistling — but with junk it's not the same. You have to have a connection, dig?

A connection. Remember the word, because to a junkie he is even more important than the junk itself. For if you don't have a connection — you have no junk. Junkies spend their lives waiting — waiting for the connection. Do you know I earned $200,000 in three years? I was at the top of the profession and my records were selling like tickets for a football game. But what did I do with those 200,000 bucks? I spent it on junk. Every penny of it. As I was always worrying about my connection, I finished by getting two or three of them in order that if one sold out on me, I could go to the other. Even then I had difficult moments. There was one time when a connection said to me, "You're not reliable, Chet. You have too many contacts. You'll have us all caught one of these days." I literally got down on my knees and begged him not to talk like that. I thought he was going to cut me out. But he turned out to be right. Sure enough one day in April 1959, when I was 30, I was picked up by the cops in a raid on a Harlem bar with two decks of junk on me.

I think I would have died if I had known exactly what it was to mean. "Three months. This time, it's a first conviction," the judge said, "but if you're caught again you'll be sent off for a long stretch." But soon I found out that those with long sentences were sent to a hospital and given their daily dose of junk while they underwent a cure. I wasn't considered that bad and they just cut off the junk on the spot and left me to lie in a cell. I had the horrors. Why I didn't die, I'll never know to this day, but I wished a

thousand times for death. You roll on the floor, you beat your head against the wall, you moan, you make animal noises, you scream. It was the end of the world. By miracle, I didn't die, and the horrors slowly went away. I had to stay in the drink for my three months; this was the longest period I'd ever been without junk or pot for many years. When I went out they called me aside, "You're cured, son," they said. "It was rough going, but now you don't need the stuff again, do you?"

"No," I said, beginning to tremble.

I seemed to be in a dream. I kept repeating to myself, "Yeah, man, now you must stay clean, clean." And then I found myself in Harlem and I went running around and collared the first connection I could find. Only once did I come around from the dream. I was in a washroom and about to jab myself with the spike. "What am I doing?" I said to myself. And then I dug it deep, ragingly, into my arm and said, "Just one fix won't hurt, man."

I wanted to give it up even at the very moment when I was spiking myself. I was now spiking myself three and even four times a day, because heroin is like that. You need more and more of it. I had no difficulty now in getting junk. I'd been in the can and hadn't squealed on the connections. They knew they could rely on me and I was earning big money with my records and playing. But I'll tell you something that should make your square's head of hair stand up on end. I left the heroin and went on to coke. And the kick you get outta snow, though stronger than the one from heroin injection, lasts a shorter time. A musician, if he wants to perform well, has to take it just before he sits down to play. But it affects your stomach — it gives you pains and makes you vomit. And with a sore stomach you can't play the horn. So here was I with a stop-watch in my hand, waiting for the right moment to sniff the stuff — the moment which was near enough to the time when I was going to play, so that I would still be getting a kick out of it, and yet not too near, so that the pains in the stomach would have passed and I would be able to blow.

I had to stop if I didn't want to be in the deathhouse in three months and somehow I did. Of course I didn't give the stuff up. But I went back from snow to heroin and then I managed almost to cut the hard stuff out. But I knew I was bound to go back to it again if I didn't get the hell outa New York. And then I heard about a lot of cats having gone to Paris, France, to play there, and so I said to Helema one day, my first wife, "Honey, pack your bag 'cause we're off to Paris." We arrived and took a pad up in Montpartnasse. I found a lot of old friends from back home and had no difficulty in getting engagements because my records were also selling well in Paris.

But things just don't work out that nice. Because here in Paris, we American cats, feeling a bit lonely as we didn't speak the lingo, would meet in each other's pads to smoke reefers and talk about the old times back in Harlem. Because I met a cat called Peter Lettman. Peter had been here longer than I had, and he had never been off the hard stuff. He passed onto me all his connections, and with the possibility of having easy fixes again, I went back on to the junk. I'd now even given up wanting to stop being a junkie. I knew the hard stuff would kill me, but I reasoned that there was nothing I could do about it, and when I felt blue about dying young, I spiked myself. I was at a party one night with several cats and among them was Dick Twardzick, an American of Polish origin. Twardzick had also been hooked by Peter Lettman and was taking the hard stuff regularly. In the middle of the party he went into the bathroom and gave himself a fix. He had already taken a shot earlier and had complained that he wasn't high. Now he gave himself an overdose. He just managed to come into the room and then went out flat on the floor. "Give him a salt shot," someone cried, but somebody else had the better idea of getting an ambulance while most of the cats present cleared out. But Twardzick was dead when they got him to the hospital. The next day, deciding that it was now or never, I went and saw a doctor. This French guy shook his head sadly. "There's nothing much I can do," he said, "you'll fight hard, you'll kick and then you'll start all over again."

At the time I felt like punching him in the nose, though now, of course, I see that he was right. "The best thing you can do is to take Palfium," he told me. "What's that?" I wasn't very keen on foreign stuff we don't use back home. "Palfium 875 is a new synthetic pain-killing substance. It's sold in tablet form, but you can crush them and mix the powder with a little water. Inject the mixture as you do with heroin. You'll find it has the same effect, but it's not habit-forming. You can buy it openly anywhere and you don't need a prescription. In time try and

reduce the doses of Palfium until you are completely cured."

Well, man, the wonder was that it worked, though I wouldn't like to say it wasn't habit-forming. I couldn't give it up. But psychologically, as you squares say, it was the end of the nightmare of shamefully running all over town for a connection. At any time of day, I could walk into a druggist

(continued on page 140)

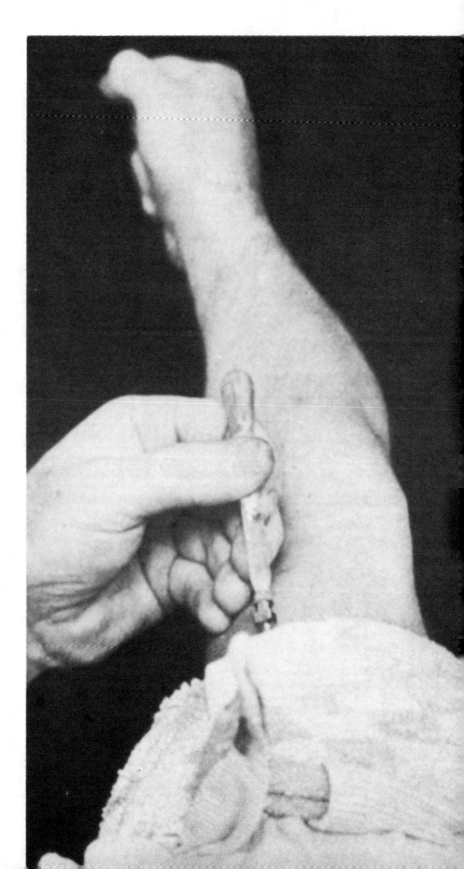

BEAT

Herbert Huncke, William Burroughs, Neal Cassady and Jack Kerouac encounter Dr. Alfred Kinsey, grey eminence of American sex research

ing OFF WiTH DR. KiNSEY

By Raymond La Scienz

What the hell was Dr. Kinsey really doing, hanging around Times Square, asking men to tell him about their sex lives, getting them to drop their drawers and measure their cocks for science?

Did you show your cock to Kinsey, Huncke? I ask, trying to imagine Kinsey himself asking the question. Herbert Huncke chuckled and nodded his head. "Well, when I found out there was something in it for me, it was a lot easier, let me tell you. But I *was* interested in the man.

"His face was, you know" — gesturing with fluttering claw about his own lined face — "very intelligent."

He wasn't a pervert? You know, there's a new group of folks attacking him as such these days.

"I don't believe so, no, but of course I assumed he was when I first heard about what he was doing. And yes," he smirked, "I know you wanna know. At one interview I did take out my cock, after he requested I do so. He wanted to know its length both flaccid and hard. So I proceeded to give myself an erection." His hands make a jerk-off motion as casually as waving hello. "In those days it was no problem."

So all those size statistics in the 1948 Kinsey study titled *Sexual Behavior in the Human Male* are based, on some relative scale, on reality. Something heartening in that simple confirmation.

At the time Huncke got to know Kinsey, the good doctor was at the tail end of his study, running out of money, and trying to convince Indiana University — the institution backing the study — to allow him to continue with his work.

(continued on page 146)

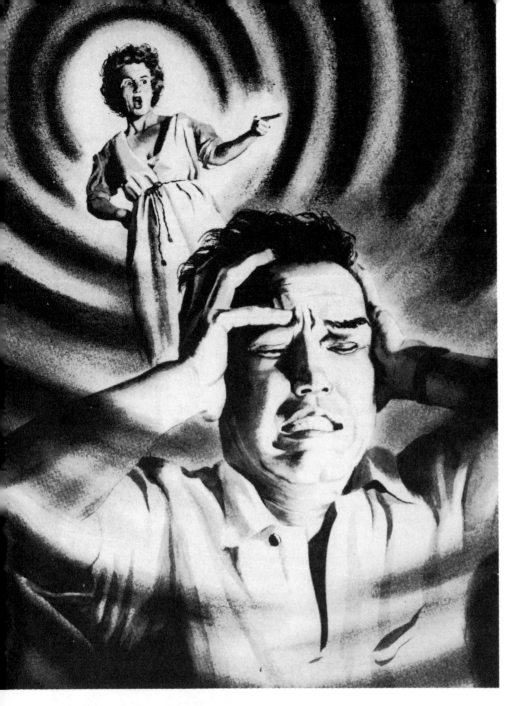

by George H. Smith

"Is your tie on straight?"

"Yes, dear," Charles Henry said, adjusting it. He was shifting from foot to the other in his eagerness to be off.

"Hold still so I can fix your collar," Agnes Henry said, leaning her sharp features close to his for a last minute inspection.

"Do you have a clean handkerchief?"

"Yes, dear." If only he could get away. If only once he could get away without the full treatment, without the complete morning routine.

"Yes, dear."

The one solace of Charles Henry's life was that he could walk out of the four-room prison he called home every morning at 8:25. That was the one thing that kept his soul alive within him. No matter how much she might want to, his wife couldn't prevent his going to work, not if she wanted to eat that is.

"Don't forget to pay the light bill."

"Yes, dear." All she could do was stand by glowering at him, repeating a seemingly endless list of instructions for the day. Sooner or later she would

have to let him go.

"And pick up my new reducing formula."

"Yes, dear." The grating, dominating voice was tearing at his mind, ripping off layer after layer of sanity.

"Yes?"

"Yes, who?"

"Yes, dear."

"That's better. And don't forget..." If only she would let him go!

"Yes, dear."

"Don't forget to pick up my ticket on the morning train for Chicago. Mother is expecting me. The poor dear, it's little enough pleasure she gets out of life since you dragged me down here."

"Yes, dear, I won't forget." A little spot of warmth began to spread through his body, warming the chill blood in his veins and starting his heart to pounding.

"And Charles..." Now it was coming. The one final humiliation, the complete subjugation of his spirit that she never forgot. But this time he didn't care, for she was really going. She was going and he would have a whole week to himself. How like her to wait until the day before to tell him. But she was really going and he had to struggle to control his face, to prevent the inward joy from showing through.

"And Charles..." She raised her voice as though she suspected that he might not be listening. "When you get to the office and take off your coat, be sure your fly is zipped up."

"Yes, dear." Once at a party he had come unzipped and he would never forget the humiliation of Agnes' harsh voice breaking into the flow of conversation. "Charles, you're unzipped!"

Never since then had she trusted him to leave the house without an investigation as to the condition of his fly. But it was almost over now. Even Agnes ran out of questions and orders finally.

"Yes, dear."

Yes, DEAR!

"Yes, dear, what? I didn't say anything."

"Yes, dear ... I mean no, dear." In just a few moments he would be free. Free for his his ten-minute walk to the station where he caught the commuter train to New York. For those ten minutes he would be his own master. For those ten minutes he could think of the week ahead, a week of doing just what he wanted and of not having to say "Yes, dear." He would just sort of amble along viewing the brightly colored houses, occasionally looking over a garden wall or stopping to watch a child playing.

"Yes, dear." When he got to the park he could watch the girls, watch the way their skirts clung to their skim hips and thighs and the way their brown and white legs flashed in the early spring sunlight. He would ...

"And Charles, you needn't be in such a hurry. I've been wondering why you're always in such a hurry in the morning. It doesn't take you ten minutes to get to the train. Why are you always in such a hurry?"

"I better go, dear. I don't want to miss my train," he said, backing toward the door, the warm glow still spreading through his body. A whole week to himself! He'd take his stamp album down from the shelf where Agnes had hidden it so that he wouldn't waste time on it and he'd work on it as long and as late as he pleased.

"Goodbye, dear," he said, kissing her dutifully. Agnes didn't say anything, she just smiled as he opened the door and stepped outside. It was a beautiful, beautiful morning, he decided, enjoying every onc of his ten precious minutes.

That evening as he hurried home, Charles's mood of suppressed happiness was still with him but it was tinged with just the slightest bit of apprehension. He was remembering the smile on Agnes' face as he had left. The only other time he had seen her smile like that was when she had wrung the neck of a chicken he had

made a pet of. It wouldn't have mattered what it was, the idea of his having a pet infuriated her.

"Pet ... what do you need a pet for?" she had asked him later, wolfing down huge bites of roast chicken. "if you must have one, what's the matter with him?"

She pointed to the hideous, spotted plaster dog that stood on a low shelf near the front door. He had always hated it, for its huge brown eyes reminded him too much of his own. It was like looking into a mirror and seeing his frustration and uselessness.

He threw off his feeling of foreboding and grinned at the dog as he took off his coat and hat. Agnes was going and that was all that mattered. She was actually going to the her mother's and leaving him to his own devices for a whole week.

"You're five minutes late," she greeted him.

"Yes, dear. I had to stop to pick up your ticket," he said, holding it out.

"Oh that," she said, yawning and pulling her heavy body from the divan on which she had been sprawled. "You'll have to turn it in and get the money back. I'm not going."

"Not going?" His hand fell to his

side and he looked blankly at the ticket that had been going to buy him seven peaceful days. "But you said you were going. Mother is expecting you."

"I've changed my mind. Mother can come here for two weeks like she did last month." She strode to the window and stood looking out. "You can send her the money, of course."

"But ... you said ..."

"Yes, Charles, what did I say?" Agnes asked, and suddenly he knew that she had never intended to go, that saying so had just been bait dangled before his eyes. For the first time in his married life he clenched his fists and took a step toward her.

"I decided not to go because I knew how much you would miss me." He could hear the smile in her voice, the same smile she had smiled that morning and the same one she had smiled over the chicken. His eyes fell on the big plaster dog and quite calmly he picked it up by its stupid head, stepped forward a few steps and brought the heavy base down on Agnes' head.

Her breath came out in a gasp and she fell to her knees, her hands reaching toward her head. He must do a

(continued on page 141)

illustration by Daniel Clowes

HEADSHRINKING
THE (DIRTY) JOKE

BY ADAM PARFREY

Remember the hey-day of the dirty joke? When leering, beehived crones with names like Rusty Warren or Belle Barth invited boozing, chain-smoking lounge lizards to "Knockers Up." When the local gym was the stage for the regaling of smutty gags, long before the Village People popularized the location as Blow-job Central. When the Elks, Moose, Knights of Columbus, Shriners or any of a number of fraternal organizations supplied the excuse for the suburban male's "night out." When *Sex to Sexty, Jokes for the John, Nugget, Jem,* and a thousand other venues for stag humor primed the pump for America's near-insatiable thirst for "off-color" humor.

It was during these halcyon days of the Borscht Belt ethos that Gershon Legman researched his comprehensive tomes on sexual humor, *Rationale of the Dirty Joke* (printed in two volumes in 1968 and 1975 respectively). *Rationale of the Dirty Joke, Series One and Two,* are candidates for the most remarkable volumes of folklore and cultural criticism to have been published in the past quarter-century. Throughout two-thousand plus pages, Legman surveys the entire range of sexual and scatological humor in an essayist format reminiscent of Robert Burton's renaissance classic, *The Anatomy of Melancholy:* original research augments opinionated and informative digressions that — though they may not always be pertinent — are endlessly fascinating.

Rationale of the Dirty Joke represents over 40 years of scrupulous research of a kind that could not be accomplished within the comfort of a public library. The majority of the four-thousand dirty jokes (plus variants) were collected "in the field" while a minority were culled from scurrilous and long-forgotten pamphlets, magazines and books (many the sort once bought by "private subscription.") We are ever in Mr. Legman's debt for documenting this essential part of our cultural heritage that seemed too declassé to merit the attention of other cultural avatars.

Born in Scranton, Pennsylvania, in 1917, Gershon Legman expatriated to the French Riviera in the late 1950s, residing in a castle that once was a stronghold of the Knights Templars. And although he was official bibliographer for the Kinsey Institute and (briefly) writer in residence at the University of California at La Jolla in the early 1960s, Legman steadfastly refused to confine his writing style and range of interests to the kind usually given approval by the academic hierarchy. It was Legman who coined the phrase "Make Love, Not War." *In Rationale of*

the Dirty Joke, he recalls his help in the invention of the modern-day vibrator: "... A vibrating dildo of milk rubber was perfected and produced in 1937 by a famous anatomical model-maker, the late Dr. Vladimir Fortunato, in New York, being connected to a vibrating scalp-massage motor. ... For my assistance in inspiring this invention, I was presented by Dr. Fortunato with the Medium size." (It should be pointed out that Gershon Legman is not a pen name; in *Dirty Joke,* Legman takes pains to correct this misconception by asserting that he is really a "tit man.") Legman's reputation as the most knowledgable expert on erotic bibliography is undisputed. *The Horn Book,* Legman's collection of essays on the weird and secretive world of erotica, is a modern classic. His vigilant amassing of sexual folklore also yielded two famous volumes on the bawdy limerick, of which the first volume is still in print.

Perhaps the most intersting aspect to G. Legman is his self-styled position as a "controversialist." *Love and Death* (1949) and *The Fake Revolt or Gangsters of the New Freedom* (1967) are vehement and hilarious rejections of contemporary American mores. It was Legman's own press (Breaking Point) that published *The Fake Revolt,* which he distributed for free, promoting it with a circular which reads: "Kind friend (or foe): If you will send me your zip cod — no money is required — I will send you my new monograph in the style of *Love and Death*: *The Fake Revolt* or, *Gangsters of the New Freedom* (unexpurgated and complete) which you may be bloody sure nobody else is going to say either as loud or as clear — or at all." *The Fake Revolt* reveals Gershon's venemous distaste for the "revolutionary" fashions of the then-burgeoning drug/hippie scene. Sample ranting sentiment: "When your wind-blown, electronic-ukelele toting, motorcycle-riding, marihuana-smoking "folksinger" or composer hears the word intellect, he too reaches for the safety-catch of his automatic, as earlier remarked by Baldur von Schirach, head of the Hitler Jugend." Legman's comparison of flower children with the Nazis is characteristic of his wild, free-form social criticism that stimulated the bone of contention among his readers while earning the wrath of Institutional scholars and critics. (In the late 1960's, an irritated Time magazine critic labeled Legman "The Joe McCarthy of queerbaiting"; the epithet was largely based upon Legman's unusual and oft-stated contention that homosexuality is the result of hatred and aggression against members of one's own sex.)

One can well understand Legman's intolerance of the

hippy movement in terms of its psychedelic threat to the booze-centric attitude to eroticism that Legman had so thoroughly documented and understood. Prior to the mainstream popularity of marihuana and LSD, alcohol was the magic potion that unshackled social inhibitions, and for this reason dirty jokes and consumption of alcohol went hand in hand. Men's magazines of the pre-psychedelic era doted on the virile and sensual virtues of alcohol to such a degree that several magazines (one titled *Cocktail* among them) were entirely devoted to recipes for mixed drinks accompanied by tease photos of scantily-clad girls.

Psychedelic culture, with its laissez-faire attitude to sex, regarded cocktail culture, with its sodden and lubricious low humor, laughably old-fashioned, a throwback to an unenlightened and hypocritical time. There were no dirty jokes in the repertoire of asexual, dadaist psychedelic humor: since everything was permitted, nothing was considered particularly *dirty* any more. With the shrewd and knowing eye of a master psychoanalyst, Legman immediately smelled a rat in hippy declarations of psychic and sexual sanity.

Legman's cynical and misanthropic moralism lends his writing the kind of irrepressible bile that is reminiscent of Ambrose Bierce or Mark Twain. Legman employs a Twainian epigram at the head of the Second Series of *Rationale of the Dirty Joke*, which collects together the *dirty* dirty jokes. Twain's quote, "The secret source of humor is not joy but sorrow; there is no humor in heaven" echoes Legman's conclusions precisely, that dirty jokes are psychopathologic responses to sexual fears, terrors, and homicidal aggressions. Among Legman's startling insights into the human compulsion for sexually-tinged joke-telling:

It is the rationalization — the attempt to make understandable, or at least believable, even endurable, if only as a "joke" — of some highly-charged neurotic situation into which the original folkteller of the tale has stumbled, or has found himself forced to live, perhaps out of his own (or her own) psychological need. The folktale or joke therefore represents a protective mechanism whereby the seriousness, and even the physical reality, of the situation can be denied and made light of, by telling it ... simply as a joke; as something allowing the accumulated tension of living this situation, or telling about it, or listening to it, to relieve itself in the harmless but necessary explosion of laughter. This is perhaps the principal function of the creation of humor, and certainly of the accepting of things as humorous, such as cuckoldry, seduction, impotence, homosexuality, castration, death, disease, and the Devil, which are obviously not humorous at all. Sexual humor is a sort of whistling in the dark, like Beaumarchais' Figaro, who "laughs so that he may not cry."

Exploring the dark underpinnings of sexual humor is the meat of Legman's discomforting argument throughout *Rationale of the Dirty Joke*. Readers of these volumes may never again regard the dirty joke in quite the same way. A common genre of dirty joke (Legman devotes an entire section to it) explores gibes about fucking women to death. Legman tells us that tellers of this genre of joke are masking some inadequacy — or fear of inadequacy — in fulfilling a woman's sexual demands combined with lust-murder retribution on the woman for being the object of the joke-teller's anxiety (!). The following joke betrays such a streak of viciousness, employing the phallus as a weapon:

A man is charged five dollars more than his previous visit to a whorehouse the week before. He complains a little to the Madame but finally decides to go upstairs with his usual girl. A while later the Madame hears pounding and screaming from the room upstairs, so she runs up to see what's going on. She sees the disgruntled customer running across the room battering the whore's belly with his hardon. So the Madame says, "What the hell are you doing?" And the man explains, "At these prices I'll make my own hole!"

Here's another example of the depraved kind of anti-woman violence disguised as a popular joke in the late 1950s:

A carpenter who has put up a partition in a whorehouse is told to "take it out in trade" when he asks for his promised thirty dollars pay. He tells the Madame that no one in the house attracts him but her. Flattered, she lies down and he puts his thumb in her vagina and his middle finger in her anus. "What do you call that?" she asks. "That's the bowling hold, you bitch," he replies. "Now give me my thirty dollars or I'll rip out your partition."

"Seriously, how do people get laughs with jokes like that?" ponders an amazed Legman over the stupidity and bestiality of the "partition" joke above. Throughout *Rationale of the Dirty Joke* we are treated to Legman's grieving comments on the psychic state of the American male as exhibited by his peculiarly sado-masochistic sense of humor. Legman's penetrating reading of the American male brainscape brings to mind David Niven's quip during an Academy Awards broadcast when a buck-naked streaker burst on-camera during the live broadcast: "Here's a man who likes to exhibit his shortcomings." A Freudian *(Rationale of the Dirty Joke* is partly modeled on Freud's pioneering *Jokes and Their Relation to the Unconscious)*, Legman believed that one could decode a personality according to his joke preference. Legman quotes Freud's description of social erotic joketelling as verbal rape:

As soon as the libidinal impulse of the first person [the man] to gratify himself through the woman, is blocked, he immediately develops a hostile attitude towards this second person [the woman], and takes the originally intruding third person as his confederate. Through the obscene speech of the first person, the woman is exposed before the third person, who now as a listener is bribed by the easy gratification of his own libido.

Legman agrees with Freud's observation that in most cases it really isn't our enemies who harm us, it's our hatred for those we love that destroys us. This hatred might be based upon insecurity over fulfilling one's wife sexually; this situation is often expressed in penis size or adultery jokes. Fears about impotence may be signaled by the joketeller's castration gag, or if expressed hostilely, jokes that employ violence against women. Fear of being overwhelmed by the female may result in vagina size or vagina dentata jokes.

A woman tells her husband that she dreamed there was an auction of pricks. Big ones for ten dollars, small ones were fifty cents. "And how much did they get for ones like mine?" asks the husband. "Oh, those they gave away for nothing." "I had a dream, too," he rejoins; "I dreamt they were auctioning off cunts. Big ones were ten dollars, and little ones were a hundred dollars." "And how much did they get for ones like mine?" "That's where they held the auction."

The way Legman categorizes *Rationale of the Dirty Joke* is a further tip-off to the neurotic content of the erotic gibe. The First Series volume includes sections on: penis envy, the primal scene, tormenting the teacher, the castratory threat, incest, pedophilia, zoöphily, purposeful perversion, rape, the sadistic concept of coitus, hostility against the penis, sexual rejection, female castration, overcompensation for impotence, adultery, funerals and mourning. And this is the clean volume. The Second Series, subtitled *No Laughing Matter,* essays the dirty dirty joke, with subsections covering: sado-masochistic homosexuality, the "short-arm" inspection, fellation as rape, rape by animals, bilking the prostitute, disease and disgust, defiling of the mother, vagina dentata, attack on the testicles, circumcision as cannibalism, self-castration, crepitation, defecation, scatophagy, and last but not least, anal sadism. Legman's astute flair for categorization goes far to prove his point that the dirty joke is a social means of coming to terms with the most repulsive and mortifying aspects of life.

At its behavioral root, the laugh may not be an expression of conviviality at all. Animal behaviorists have noted the similarity of the laugh, with its open-mouthed, teeth-bared expulsion of sound, to postures of confrontation. Some playwrights have used to striking effect the laugh as an ironic replacement for the cry of agony or terror. Today's situation comedy mania may be a tip-off to some deeply-harbored national psychosis that demands numbingly constant iteration.

Legman explains the development of "sick" humor in American culture as a response to a sick culture, whose most grandiose achievement is the detonation of the atomic bomb, or as Legman calls it, a "mushroom-shaped fecal explosion":

There has developed over the last thirty years, particularly in America, this use of ... comedy-insanity far beyond what was formerly understood as the humor of "fools," or even of the sacred wandering Bedlam lunatics ... and the dwarfed and disturbed characters who have always classically been — and still are — the court-jesters, circus clowns, carnival geeks, and nightclub and vaudeville ... comedians, all of whom have specifically in common their allowed and open expression of all the uglier ... parts of their own and the audience's id.

Because it confronts us with so many unpleasant truths about the reality of our psychological health, Gershon Legman's *Rationale of the Dirty Joke* is an unsettling but essential read. Legman's challenging insights combined with his prodigious feat of folklorist scholarship illumine us on mysteries of the human mind we would like to keep secret, even from ourselves.

A man in an upper berth on a train is watching an old maid undressing in the berth below. She unscrews a wooden arm, wooden leg, takes off her wig, removes false teeth, and a glass eye. Suddenly she sees the man watching her. "What do you want?" she cries. "You know damn well what I want," he says. "Unscrew it and throw it up here."

June Wilkinson dances for You

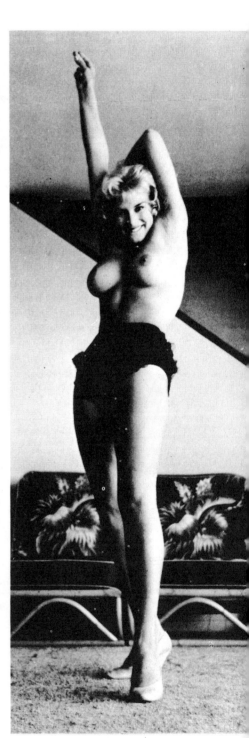

SOUNDS of seduction

By Dick Blackburn

The pounding of the drums ... in their blood. Through the noise the sex-madness, the half-drunken dancers ... Syncopated passion screaming with lust, the drums horribly primitive; drunken embraces ... orgiastic music — beautiful hideous! ... Flushed faces, breaths hot with passion and whiskey... On and on, the drunken carnival to maddening music — the passion, the lust!

A black magic voodoo orgy in the forest? *Au contraire mon chere frere.* Merely a college dance from a 1924 sub-Fitzgeraldian bestselling college novel *(The Plastic Age* by Percy Marks). As would happen later with booting r&b in the 50s, le jazz hot gets unfairly jacketed as a gonad-zapping afro-disiac. A very square misconception. Experienced roués who utilize music for a sensual mood know that frantic is fine for the dance floor — it warms the corpuscles. But when you hit the couch the tempo, along with the lights, must be lowered. Women are more inclined to come across when their senses are stroked not shaken!

Naturally, you are well on your way to a score if the lady in question digs your selection, whatever it is, from the get go. But that's a gamble unless you know her tastes. Better to pick something that bypasses her intellectual prejudices and mellows her out before she can pass judgement. Popular is too risky. She's bound to have an opinion on it and if it's negative you've lost points. Obscure is good. If she's never heard of it she doesn't know if she's supposed to like it or not. But listen up you avant-gardists! Obscure does not mean weird. She shouldn't pay more attention to the music than she does to you. You want it merely to slip past her consciousness and gently massage her cortex. Nothing abrasive, nothing overly attention-getting.

Of course once you know her you can slant you selection to her individual personality. Before that use caution. However you can't just pick anything smooth and hope it goes down a treat. Use your head, Fred. You wouldn't play Tony Bennett for an Elvis-fascinated bopper.

Tap the imagination! Granted there's no easy answers. I've been trying to come up with the right formula since high school. Back then Santo and Johnny, the Fleetwoods and the breathy Paris Sisters doing "I Love How You Love Me" were all top faves but, good as they were, still a little too vox polpuli. And I refused to play Johnny Mathis, the boringly ubiquitous *sine qua non* of the would-be make out artiste. I wanted to come across as suavely elegant - not easy for a gangly teen. So I took to softening up puritanical defences with Chopin waltzes until I felt the moment was ripe to segue into the mounting strains of Ravel's "Bolero." Gauche, I admit, but in those more innocent times I enjoyed a few successes.

Later in college, Miles Davis' Columbia lp's like "Miles Ahead," "Sketches of Spain" and "Kind Of Blue" were all in my collection, as was his outing on Prestige "Jazz for Lovers" (all still effective, all still available). It was then I learned that responses to music could be affected by a women's geography or even religion. I began to fine tune. For a sentimental Houman, Louisiana native I played the yearning swamp pop ballads of her native bayou land, and, after initially striking out with a lapsed catholic coed, I turned off Astrud Gilberto and Stan Getz, lit candles and put on Gregorian Chants. Eh, voila!

'Course I've had my share of flameouts too. Early dixieland sounded to one woman like "Bear Country Jamboree at Disneyland" and Don Williams (probably the best C&W choice) was unacceptable to another because it reminded her of "guys in bars without any teeth and wet comb-backed hair" — an unhappy image from her childhood. Be alert to these unexpected quirks and flexible enough to re-think in midstream.

Okay. The fireplace is blazing and the post prandial cocktails have been poured. You turn to your turntable/cassette deck/CD player and put on ... what?

My first choice would be unaccompanied guitar. It's the warmest, sexist, most romantically intime sound around. Classical Spanish is best. Segovia, Laurindo Almeida, Julian Bream. Of course if your lady is on the bold side you can mix in some flamenco. Try Montoya, Manitas de Plata and Paco de Lucia. If you want homegrown go with John Fahey. "Of Rivers And Religion" on Warners is out of print but if found will induce that same "enternity-held-in-a-note" trance-like state.

Next to the guitar the sax has the most caressing sound. "After Hours," a smoky r&b instro comp from King has just been reissued with both instuments spotlighted by a succession of great players like Earl Bostic, Pet "Guitar" Lewis, etc. Two of Ellington's alumni are maestros of the ballad. On alto, Johnny Hodges and on tenor Ben Webster. For Hodges try the small group recordings from the late 30s / early 40s. "Night Wind" may be the prettiest thing he never did but is hard to locate. Webster's outing on Pablo with Art Tatum is especially sensuous. And ex-Basie sideman Lester Young's proto-cool sound is heard to good advantage on Blue Note's collection of his Aladdin sides.

Speaking of Lester, you shouldn't ignore his soulmate Billie Holiday, or "Lady Day" as he called her. Most everything she sang in that insinuating nasal style, the notes stretched, swallowed and poured in your ear like warm honey, is fine. But the *créme de la créme* were the sides cut for Commodore and later re-released on Atlantic. Also check out Lil Green on RCA. She was bluesier than Holiday but with a similar style. "Romance in The Dark" and "Knockin' Myself Out (Slowly By Degrees)" supported by Big Bill Broonzy's masterful single string playing, are classics.

Another vocalist with that burnished tone is Charles Brown (king of west coast cocktail lounge blues). His throaty, plaintive style is timeless. Just the first few notes will make your girl want to shed her shoes. In the same late 40s time frame are fellow California crooners Ivory Joe Hunter and Little Willie Littlefield. All are reissued on the import label Route 66.

If these become too difficult to glom you can always go with Nat King Cole or Ol' Blue Eyes himself. In the flick *The Baby Maker*, sexy young hippy Barbara Hershey tells a suburban couple that they "have a lot of Frank Sinatra" to which the hubby replies "We have all the Beatles too." Nowadays they're both institutions and the us vs. them division has disappeared. The Capitol albums (not the new box set — too many ring-a-dingers!) like "Wee Small Hours," "Where Are You" and "For the Lonely" prove Sinatra to be the greatest saloon singer ever.

Old vocal group reissues of The Flamingos, Moonglows, Spaniels, Orioles are fine too. In fact most of the older music is preferable to the new when in the clinches except If you're into a May/December thing and don't want the nubile young lady pegging you for a moldy fig. In that case try Michael Rother, Phillip Glass or any of the New Music boys. And since international music is au courant you might pick up something lush from the Third World like the tangos of Astor Piazzola.

Here's another movie quote, this time from the hallowed *Sweet Smell Of Success.* "How many drinks," purrs weasel Sidney Falco of B-girl Barbara Nichols, "does it take to get you into that tropical island mood?" But you can let your loudspeakers put you in the island itself which will encase you and your targeted demoiselle in a cocoon of permissiveness. The most famous practitioner of Naugahyde exotica is Martin Denny who, if you don't want to search through second hand record bins, has a "best of" recently reissued on Rhino. Bring on the tiki torches!

Yma Sumac's reissued lp's, although well worth checking out on their own extraterrestrial merits, are too genuinely bizarre unless you're romancing Rima the Bird Girl. Her trills and guttural whoops suggest less a jungle paradise that a headhunter attack. Better to go with the sound of Los Calchakis (their oft-performed folk melody "El Condor Pasa" was copped by third world fan Paul Simon for his "Bridge Over Troubled Water"). Listening to their otherworldly guitar and wooden flute from high in the Andes can cause lightheadedness as if one had ingested too much thin air. Especially effective on women who don't imbibe.

A word about your sound system. We've come a long way from *Pillow Talk,* when Rock Hudson activated a stack of schmaltzy lp's from a wall switch. Now we have remote controls to fade volume, reprogram, and repeat play all from your seat of action. These must, however, be used with CD players. The changers will give you the longest time — over a hundred selections but then you are forced to listen inevitably to everything on each CD and not all the cuts may fit the mood. A 90 minute cassette holds about forty selections but of your own choosing! An important consideration. Also you can have it automatically repeat for as long as you need it to do so. To my mind an aurally customized seduction shows greater care, planning and independence of taste to the prospective seductee. But if you haven't the time and/or inclination for it, the CD changer is definitely the way to go.

So, with this as a rudimentary guide, you are now prepared to make a stealthy sonic assault on the object of your desires.

Bwana Fortuna!

Space Age Bachelor Pad Music

Imagine what George Jetson would be like if he hadn't married Jane. Hubba-hubba! Imagine Leroy Anderson's "Syncopated Clock" played by Perez Prado. Yessir, we're talking about the decadent, easy-livin', modern convenience world of Space-Age Bachelor Pad Music.

The world's *premier* authority on Space-Age Bachelor Pad Music (which, from now on, we'll term SABPM) is Byron Werner, who was interviewed for *CAD* by Jerry Nutter, editor/publisher of *Audio Carpætorium* (111-32 112th Street-SOP, NY 11420-1026), a magazine that plumps for the now-forgotten virtues of analog recording and hi-fi equipment.

How did you come by coining the phrase, "Space-Age Bachelor Pad Music?"

You have to understand the antecedents of SABPM. It came out of the Exotica trend, which was itself an extension of the Latin music trend, which was influenced by the War in the Pacific rest and recreation dream. After the Latin and Exotica craze ran its course, the record companies were trying to find the next big thing. They had new instruments like the theremin, and invented a whole bunch of new studio tricks — stereo was then a novelty. What with the space race and the rise of science fiction, men found the outer limits of exotic. Science Fiction exotic, which was even more exotic than the exotic locales on earth.

This was really a white male thing, wasn't it?

Definitely. You can always tell a lot more about the people making the exotic music than the supposed inspiration for the exotic music itself. You can tell what was appealing to them. Overblown, wacky arrangements. Percussion spectaculars. There was a record, "Zounds, What Sounds!" that exemplifies the entire SABPM obsession. It was the percussion arrangement record taken to a whole new level, the kind that would get used as a demonstration in stereo stores, for example.

What turns an otherwise ordinary "mood record" into music for a space-age bachelor pad?

Use of a theremin, sound effects, discordant harmonies, exaggerated stereo panning, zippy, optimistic melodies.

What is the distinction between the Exotica records of Martin Denny, Les Baxter and Arthur Lyman, and the SABPM craze?

Exotica was for ex-servicemen to conjure up fantasies of the South Sea Island beauties. And for bachelors who used them for romance and seduction. Those records by and large had a calming effect. SABPM is just the opposite. Go baby go, wow wow wow! It's like a guy in his sports car. A guy is going to floor it and a woman's going to baby it. Single guys are the ones who are most involved in the stereo sets, how it sounded — uppity music to get the juices flowing. For the most part, I think women of the day found it annoying, irritating. Too jumpy. It's still that way with a lot of young men's music.

So the fans of SABPM were guys with too much disposable income?

Lonely guys with too much disposable income who are nit-picky about their stereos!

Yeah, in the late 50s and early 60s, the stereo version of an lp cost a dollar more than the mono one. And prerecorded open reel tapes were a stratospheric $7.95 and up!

And these records are ideal for showing off your stereo… They're not any good for dancing, like Latin music, or seducing, like Jungle music, or anything else, but showing off that new hi-fi set.

Owning a hi-fi in the 50s meant a lot more than it does nowadays. The modern equivalent would probably be owning a satellite dish. But what else defines the category, Byron? Does it have to be instrumental?

Well, it helps. The vocalizing that seems to typify SABPM

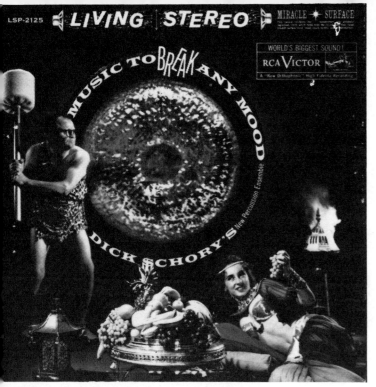
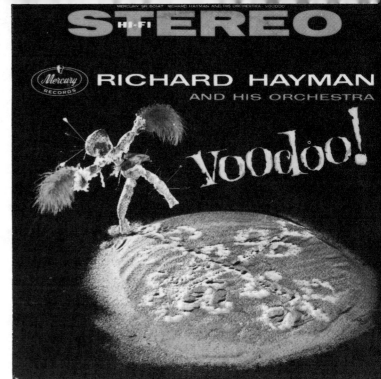

is a wordless "zu-zu-zu-zu" kind of singing, best heard on records by Juan Garcia Esquivel, the king of SABPM music.

I'm thinking of Perez Prado's recording of "Cherry Pink and Apple Blossom White" ....

"Cherry Pink and Apple Blossom White" is one of his more commercial hits. Once it hits that opening riff, it makes all the older folks (my parent's generation) go "Aaaaah!" Myself, I like his screwier numbers like "Monitor Mambo" and "Marilyn Monroe Mambo." I don't consider him in with SABPM, but an important influence on it.

Don't you think that the guys who bought into SABPM were already too old to get into rock when it came along? So, when something like "Dawn of Dylan" by Hugo Montenegro appeared, they bought into it to appear hip?

The rock that was around at the time of SABP music was more in the line of Elvis and that ilk. These guys had no interest in rock at all. "Dawn of Dylan" came much later and probably fits more readily into Irwin Chusid's "Atrocious Music" than into SABPM.

Who's your favorite performer in the SABPM genre?

The number one performer has got to be Esquivel. Esquivel's the king. He had all these crazy, space-age arrangements. For the vocal groups particularly. The music was very overt, with only an occasional subtlety. It sort of tickles you with a feather, then hits you with a hammer. Quiet, then very loud.

How 'bout some other noted practitioners?

I like Bob Thompson a lot. He did such albums as "Just for Kicks," "Mmmm Nice!" "On the Rocks." They're all on RCA. Then there's Henri René. He was into the quiet-loud, quiet-loud arrangements. Harry Revel, he's another.

Did SABPM have its own evolution?

Certainly! SABPM went right into the early weird Moog stuff, like Perry-Kingsley's "In Sounds From Way Out" and Dick Hyman moog arrangements. I should also mention Martin

Denny's "Exotic Moog" album, the grandaddy of the cheezy synthesizer sound.

Can you describe the process whereby a rock record collector drifts into SABP music? You could have more easily gone back to doo-wop, blues, or western swing, because the markets for these categories are well-established. You can't walk into Tower Records and ask them where the Space-Age Bachelor Pad section is! Did it have anything to do with hunting for records at thrift stores, and not finding what you're looking for, and taking a chance on something else which looked interesting?

I often buy records solely by their cover illustrations. I never ask the store operators for this stuff. The most I will ask is, "Any Easy Listening?" Of course they sneer ... let 'em! I get more enjoyment out of a 50¢ "garbage" record than they will out of a stack of current compact disks. I never know what I want 'till I see it, anyway.

Can you tell us what to look for when hunting for SABPM records?

A cover with a dolled-up babe is the best tip-off for SABPM stuff. And I look for Easy Listening in used record stores that specialize in rock. Chances are, if they have an Easy Listening section they couldn't care less about it and charge next to nothing. Salvation Army and thrift store records are usually far too scratchy to even bother with. Swap meets are best. I can't tell you how many turkeys I've bought to find the occasional gem. These records are few and far between.

I imagine you'd agree that any album entitled: "New Sounds Hi-Fi," "Stereo Demonstration," "The (insert your choice) Singers," or "Somebody-You-Never-Heard-Of Plays the Hits of Today on the Zither" would be worth a dollar or two of your hard-earned dough.

I don't like to spend over a dollar.

You get more bang for the buck that way.

Let's face it: Nearly everyone still considers this stuff worse than garbage.

KING OF THE 'B's

Miss Henks: Debra Lamb

Mr. Gurney: Larry Wessel

Photographer: Scott Lindgren

My, my, Miss Henks. Right on time!

Nice credentials ya got there!

We got to see if they're real!

My, my, my! You're perfect for the part.

Did you read the fine print?

Hands off, Mr. Gurney!

Velma
warned me
about
you!

My, my, Miss Henks!
Quite the marksman, too!

There is no other sight in the world like that of a beautiful woman about to be whipped.

Not a delicate blonde, petite and subject to fainting, but a tall, dangerous brunette, full-figured and with a strong will.

You know the type: a cross between Romy Schneider and Sophia Loren. At a frequent habitat like where you work, she may earlier have taunted you by just plain being around too much. And now she hangs before you, stripped and spread-eagled. Perhaps she is suspended by chains and breathless in either the privacy of your living room or a local dungeon.

Her widening eyes seek and anticipate the action of the instrument you hold in your hands: three feet of horsehair, hemp, or leather bound to a small hollow stock of bamboo (to ensure a more direct swish). You slowly lift it, and then surprise her once with a quick, soft flash across her naked belly. A shiver passes and the eyes close in ecstacy, but before she can completely tense and prepare her muscles now minutely dotted with sweat, you follow with the inevitable and, at your will, lash her bare back, breasts and shoul-

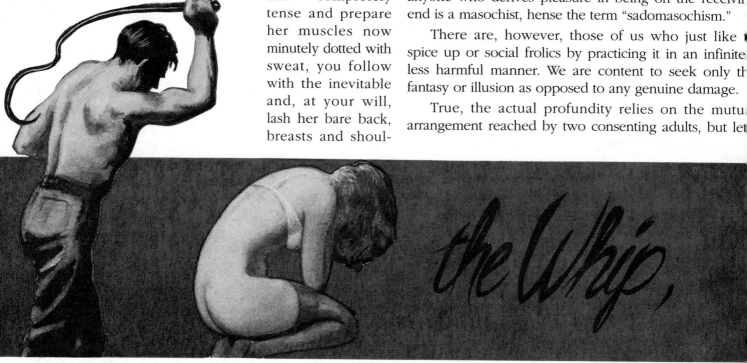

ding crop craze" had formerly been your pleasure to d[i]cover in her, keep it to yourself. What was good for y[ou] may result in outright injury to someone else; this is [a] sensitive "kink" to be approached with caution.

It is an absurdly pompous fact that flogging for fu[n] has been diversion passionately indulged in for man[y] centuries by everyone from Royalty to ragamuffin. Ey[e]brows of scholarly and simple man alike would rise [at] the sight of a sound, public whipping. When it was ov[er] they would leave for their home or brothel (hot bloo[d] still pounding in their temples) and attempt to continu[e] the humor with wife or strumpet.

As a result, thousands of games, excuses, and varia[a]tions of frivolous flagellation came to be whispere[d] about everywhere from the preacher's pulpit to Peru. B[ut] in the bedroom or not, the joy wasn't always so mutu[al] and the recipient of the lash often suffered.

So much for the good old days.

To put it plainly, anyone who derives pleasure [in] inflicting pain or injury to his fellow man is a sadist. A[nd] anyone who derives pleasure in being on the receivin[g] end is a masochist, hense the term "sadomasochism."

There are, however, those of us who just like [to] spice up or social frolics by practicing it in an infinite[ly] less harmful manner. We are content to seek only th[e] fantasy or illusion as opposed to any genuine damage.

True, the actual profundity relies on the mutu[al] arrangement reached by two consenting adults, but let[']s

ders, although you needn't stop there.

For many healthy couples the world over, it is the ultimate "slap and tickle" where foreplay is concerned.

Once a fling has flung and your now ex-girl decides she wants to see someone else, you might be a good sport about it and for better results, tip off the new guy to a few of her intricacies. These are trifles ranging from simple "blow in her ear" to the more bovine "scratch her belly" variety (the latter being, of course, that special type of intimacy she'd be least likely of your disclosing to forgive).

But if it was that a "lash lust," "birch binge," or "rid-

be honest: utter brutality and bleeding lacerations rarel[y] contribute to the makings of "a good time." When prop[e]rly staged, the mere charade of corporal punishmen[t] can be thrilling enough and, to a true sadist, prove [a] thumping bore.

A mild enough perversion to be sure, entire volume[s] can be written on whippings primeval release of stres[s] and anxiety after a hard day's work.

Usually, the average guy can gauge his partner's wi[ll] to submission through any number of hints. For example:

1. How well does she respond to love taps?

2. Does she smile during prison films, sword & sandal epics, or Zorro adventures and why?

3. Does her book library include ANY work by the Marquis de Sade?

If, during heated moments of lovemaking laced with tomfoolery, she exhibits a sudden disposition towards wrestling and heavy breathing, then she shares the common desire of many a woman to be secretly "conquered" by the man of her choice. Since "conquer," here, should go hand-in-hand with "protect," stay as gentle as you are macho.

And secondly, avoid devastating embarrassment by making damned sure that she doesn't conquer you.

At any rate, you've already had a few drinks and decided on your place that evening. Upon entering your den of iniquity, she may coyly comment or turn a sly eye towards a pulley here, a rope or chain there. You smartly raise one eyebrow and here the conversation turns either oddly comic or hot and heavy. Finally, she admits vaguely or otherwise to being a willing submissive and here is where steely control of your saliva flow is of the utmost. For a couple's first time the attitude should be of a cool, almost arrogant, indifference. Terrific awkwardness can ensue should one or the other appear too over-anxious.

Fastening your partner to a chair with handcuffs, as anyone into bondage can tell you, is perhaps the most simple and basic of positions. Seated regularly, her wrists are bound with two separate sets of cuffs, one on

center so you might be free to walk around and peruse the subject better.

For the more dramatic dominant, a standing position of often preferred, spread-eagled or with a single pully securing her wrists over the head.

She should, however, NEVER BE TOO HELPLESS. If you use ropes or cords, make sure she can easily slip out of them. The same goes with manacles, bonds, and handcuffs.

Sex boutiques and magic shops (!) carry a fine array of non-confining cuffs and bonds. If the real thing must be used, be sure she has easy access to the keys. Should you pass out due to euphoria or an outright coronary, this tip can be providential for all parties.

UNDER THE LASH

To paraphrase Christopher Fry, "The lady's not for whipping." Unless you are a skilled bullwhip artist and adept in mastering otherwise delicate stunts, make no mistake: potential hazard here reigns supreme. Those of us who spent some years alone in the fine art of encircling the female torso with a long, genuine whip can come in contact with the flesh and have it crack with no injury or even slight discomfort. If you have a real bullwhip gathering dust in the top of your closet and are not capable in this fashion, DON'T EVEN THINK OF IT.

A horsehair whip, the type tropical personalities employ to whisk away flies and mosquitoes, can safely be applied to most any fair maid's person without trou-

the Bed, (...and your girlfriend's bod)

by Roderick Thorndyke

each side of the chair and secured to the top of the left and right back legs just under the seat. Lower her dress or blouse down around her shoulders so that they are bare and susceptible to whatever lash you have in mind. This can prove subtly exquisite should she happen to possess the classic pulchritude of a swimmer.

Should you wish to bring the additional broadness of her back into play, simply secure her with her legs straddling the back of the chair which, unless it is comfortably cushioned, is covered with a towel for her to press her chest against as she should be topless here.

If your room is relatively large, situate her in the

ble. They come in a wide variety and are found at dealers carrying African artifacts or sex boutiques.

A several-thronged leather whip (also found at said boutique) can also be used providing your partner is of stouter stock.

For close contact (like when in bed), a large, soft leather riding crop with a short handle is ideal. The loop at the end should be somewhat wide enough to sound out a pleasing clap when laid on.

Secure (and here I use the word loosely) her wrists to the binding fastened to either side of you bed. A soft,

(continued page 144)

the world's sexiest cars

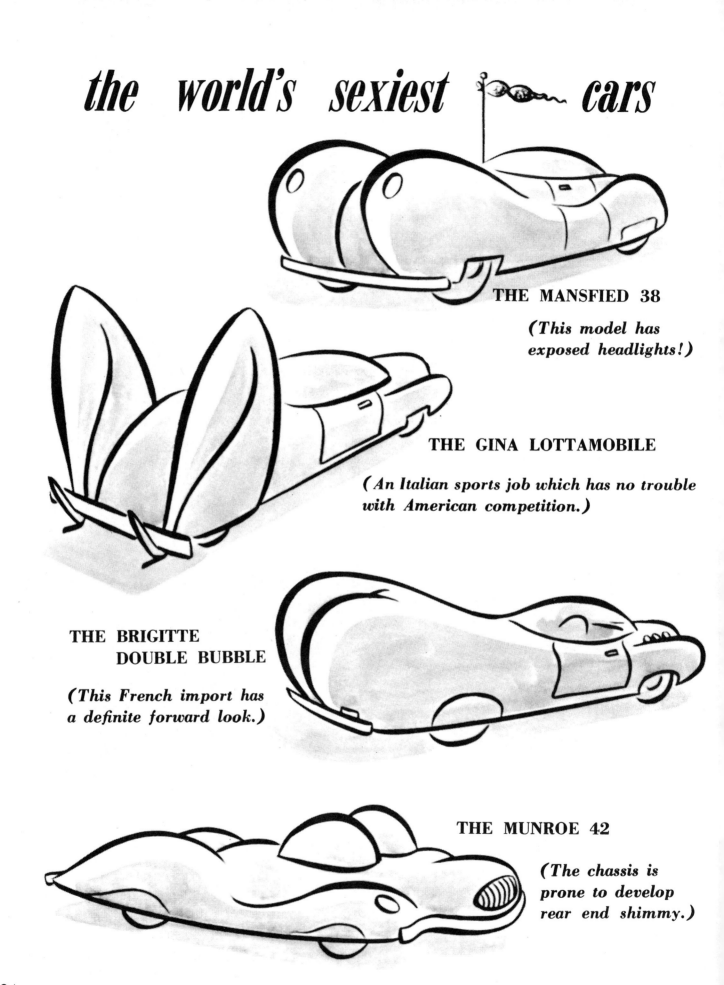

THE MANSFIED 38

(This model has exposed headlights!)

THE GINA LOTTAMOBILE

(An Italian sports job which has no trouble with American competition.)

THE BRIGITTE DOUBLE BUBBLE

(This French import has a definite forward look.)

THE MUNROE 42

(The chassis is prone to develop rear end shimmy.)

FETISHES!

by Dick Vas Deferens, M.D.

•"Case No. 81: The patient, a lawyer, age 26, was in the habit of catching live flies and pressing them to his penis while masturbating; squashing of the insect, orgasm and ejaculation — all these joined into one climactic experience." [Wilhelm Stekel, *Patterns of Psychosexual Infantilism*, p. 261.]

•"Case No. 38: Mr. G.F., 37, an engineer. A woman's kiss leads to orgasm if it is accompanied by the strange taste sensation of pus or blood. Women with bad teeth, especially if they have dentures, give him this sensation. A beautifully shaped mouth full of perfect teeth leaves him cold, while the mere thought of a denture causes sexual excitement." [Stekel, *Patterns of Psychosexual Infantilism*, p. 169.]

•"Case No. 49: A most singular case of my observation concerns a woman who suffers from a fetishism of collar buttons. Her basic feeling is and intense hatred of these articles, and she is greatly irritated both by the sight of such buttons and also of the rings which their pressure so frequently leaves in the skin. But if her sexual appetite is aroused by a man ... her fear of the buttons and her aversion to men transforms itself into a passionate curiosity to see them. She would like to put them in her mouth if possible and destroy them in her mouth." [Hirschfeld, *Sexual Pathologie*, Volume III, quoted by Stekel, *Sexual Aberrations*, Volume I, p. 300.]

• "Case No. 29: A married but childless man of about 45, impotent and separated from his wife, had for some time been collecting all kinds of colored hats and student's and fraternity caps... It was after his separation from his wife (which was due to his impotence) that he had begun to collect the caps. Whenever he would see such colored headgear, he would be overpowered by the desire to possess it, and whenever he would look over his collection of caps, he became sexually provoked, would get an erection and immediately orgasm." [Stekel, *Sexual Aberrations*, Volume I, p. 190.]

One man's turn-on, another man's — lizard food? Why be content with a pretty face and a handful of tit?

Tune in to some of these peculiar pecker picker-uppers: squashed flies, fraternity caps, collar buttons, bad teeth, found in the case histories of Richard von Krafft-Ebing and Wilhelm Stekel are an absolutely mind-blowing collection of psychoneurotic conditions the flesh is heir to.

Krafft-Ebing, the pioneering professor of perversion, preceded and influenced the leading sex researchers of this century, such as Havelock Ellis (*Studies in the Psychology of Sex*), Magnus Hirschfeld (the self-styled "Einstein of Sex") and Sigmund Freud and his entire school, which included Wilhelm Stekel, who in a couple dozen phone-book-thick tomes compiled the straight skinny on the sexually insane. These sex researchers exploded a bomb into territory the medical establishment had wished into nonexistence for 1,000 years.

The charge ignited with the first edition, in German, of Krafft-Ebing's *Psychopathia Sexualis* in 1891. Despite the author's use of arcane technical language and descriptions of sexual acts in Latin in its first German edition, the medical community collectively shit its pants. The unbelievably explicit descriptions of sexual perversion not only defied credulity, but also good taste, good sense and

any remaining vestige of Victorian libido control as wel In 1893 *The British Medical Journal* actually debate whether or not to even review the English translation c this landmark work by the famous neurologist, who ha previously authored the definitive textbook on psychiatr "We have considered at length whether we should notic this book or not, but we deem the importance of the sul ject and the position of the author make it necessary t refer to it in consideration of the feelings with which i has been discussed by the public. We have questione whether it should have been translated into English a all."

• "Case No. 229: In a provincial town a man wa caught in intercourse with a hen. He was 30 years olc and of high social position. The chickens had been dyin one after another, and the man causing it had been 'wan ed' for a long time. To the question of the judge, as to th reason for such an act, the accused said that his genita were so small that coitus with women was impossible Medical examination showed that actually the genital were extremely small. The man was mentally quit sound." [Krafft-Ebing, *Psychopathia Sexualis*, p. 375.]

Krafft-Ebing doesn't let on how he counseled thi unfortunate man, but you can be sure he wouldn't hav suggested employing a larger barnyard mate or spankin his monkey as alternatives, for the good doctor believec as most of his contemporaries, that masturbation itself le to madness. Krafft-Ebing went so far as to believe chroni masturbation a genetic malady, passed on through th generations as a predisposition for "premature manifesta tions of sexual instinct."

• "One girl masturbated shamelessly and almost cor stantly at the age of three. Another girl began at the ag of eight, and continued to practice masturbation whe married, and even during pregnancy. She was pregnar 12 times. Five of the children died early, four were hydro cephalic, and two boys began to masturbat — one at the age of seven, the other at th age of four." [Krafft-Ebing, *Psychopathia Sexi alis*, p. 37.]

Krafft-Ebing hypnotized his patients t combat the "evils" of masturbation and homc sexuality. Swinging his pocket watch, h would have certain patients repeat, "I abhc onanism, because it makes me weak and mis erable. I no longer have an inclinatio towards men; for love for men is against reli gion, nature and law. I feel an inclinatio toward woman; for woman is lovely and desirable, and created for man." On a particu larly swishy patient, Krafft-Ebing claime complete success when he learned that th patient "sought the address of a brothel."

Twenty years after the first publication c masturbation-negative *Psychopathia Sexuali* Wilhelm Stekel authored a pamphlet, *Absti nence and Health*, which examined, as Steke

wrote in his autobiography, "the exaggerated fear regarding the consequences of masturbation. What had erroneously been considered a detrimental effect of masturbation was actually the result of a mental conflict created by the much-maligned sexual activity."

Despite the best psychiatric credentials (Stekel co-edited a psychiatric journal with Freud), Stekel's outpour of tomes on sexual perversity provoked hoots of derision from within and outside the psychiatric community. *Sadism and Masochism, Sexual Abberations, Peculiarities of Behavior, Patterns of Psychosexual Infantilism, Frigidity in the Woman, Impotence in the Male* — all chock-full of the bizarre convolutions of thwarted and excessive libido, proving again and again that truth is stranger that fiction. Despite their scientific context, some cases come off like a dirty French novel. Did you hear the one about the sex-crazed broad who'd orgasm hundreds of times a day — and call it a nightmare? Stekel excerpts her diary in *Peculiarities of Behavior:*

On the street I had to fight very strongly against my fantasies. I could never plainly make out what I was daydreaming about. I felt as if I were in a trance. At the same time I experienced and endless number of orgasms. I had a vague notion that this interfered with the with the enjoyment of sexual intercourse with my husband. I did not care to have orgasms through my fancy-weaving. But I did not know how to prevent it. Every time I went out, I was in torture. The moment I left the threshold of my house, I felt an orgasm coming on. I was afraid to keep going because I felt my excitation increasing with every step. Nothing helped — in a short time I had the orgasm. Trying to suppress the orgasm proved torturous. I grew highly excited, my whole body trembled, and a troublesome restlessness seized me. Usually I went out to do shopping, but as soon as I entered a store my inner agitation would drive me out again. The onset of the orgasm, which I tried to avoid, made it impossible for me to remain on one spot for any length of time. Consequently, I could neither stand nor sit still. I had to move back and forth all the time. I could hardly tarry long enough to be waited on ... If I went to a number of stores, running back and forth, I was able to withhold the orgasm for a time;

that was as much as I was able to accomplish. Matters grew worse; I became sexually roused as soon as I began preparing to go out; indeed, soon matter came to such a pass that I began to feel sexual excitation the moment I got up from my seat. Finally, every change of posture induced an excitation within my vagina so that I did not dare get off the chair to walk around my room... [Stekel, *Peculiarities of Behavior*, pp. 49-50.]

Stekel's sleuthing reveals the source of this woman's irksome orgasms in the repression of a wild fuck she had had with her brother years before. At first, the woman orgasmed in the street around men who resembled her brother; later, merely the anticipation of such a moment would set her off.

If some episodes read like an Olympia Press meat-beater, others recall filthy borscht-circuit schtick at its lowest. Could the psychiatric community suppress a laugh at Krafft-Ebing's Case No. 211, a middle-aged transvestite and chronic masturbator who enjoyed nothing more than dipping his cock and balls in jars of milk? Krafft-Ebing adds, with a note of distaste, that the man was "cynical enough" to sell the dick-dipped mammary juice to customers at his wife's milk shop.

You know it's a tip-off for a juicy case study when the patient is severely religious or pious. In *The Psychology of Sex*, Havelock Ellis points our that "the ascetic performs exactly the same acts as are performed in these excesses

(continued on page 144)

Lady Bullfighter

by Patricia McCormick

"Are the bulls big?" I ask Martin, who is lacing my soft Spanish leggings.

"Big enough," he answers. Martin, who is my sword handler, does not like to talk about the bulls just before I am to fight them. Martin is a worrier.

"They'd better be," I say, a little resentful that Martin might be happier if the animals I am to meet were tame cows with blunt horns instead of bulls of caste, with centuries of breeding to fit them for this afternoon's spectacle. I get more satisfacation from a fight if the bulls are large.

Martin gets up and opens the door for Alejandro. I have a moment of envy as he appears in his glittering traje de luces (suit of lights), the ancient costume of the torero, little changed from the days when Spanish noblemen were the principle fighters of bulls. As he smiles confidently at me, searching for signs of anxiety on my part, I have a momentary regret that I am a woman and wear the comparatively drab costume of the Andalusian countryman. And I remember that, except for the human animal, it is the male who wears colorful plumage and that it is primarily a man's world in which I will perform this afternoon.

A bugle breaks the silence and the tunnel door opens. There is complete silence in the ring and all eyes look at the blackness the open door has exposed. My anxiety increases to the point of exasperation when nothing comes from that darkness. What is the trouble? Have the men fumbled the inner gates? Could it be that the bull does not want to venture into the brilliant sun to challenge anything he meets? I think of the difficult and cowardly bulls I have met before, bulls which would not charge frankly, per-

mitting good work; bulls which stood completely on the defensive so that I have had to carry the fight to them on every pass. It is the brave bull, the bull which challenges everything in his way, which permits a good fight. The bull comes out, not charging defiantly, but rather cautiously, investigating. The bull — not a large one — looks, takes a step or two toward the enticing cape, and halts, pawing the ground — usually the sign of bluff rather than a desire to fight.

I shake the cape in front of him as he looks at me. I call to him, coaxingly, "Hey-hey, bonita. Mira! Mira!" I have to step out firmly again and lightly shake the cape, still calling more sharply before he will attack. He passes, not charging hard but sort of hopping. I hastily search my knowledge for the best means to teach him to follow the cape and charge more frankly. He is not beautiful at all, but a difficult animal who wants to wait rather than try to throw everyone out of the ring. I can walk away from this one, all right, but there is no emotion, no appearance of dangerous contempt in my going, for the bull is not interested and everyone knows he has no intention of attacking or pursuing me. I literally have to chase him! I decide to kill him quickly.

When I go to the barrera for the killing sword, Alejandro warns me that he's bad to the right. That is the horn I have to clear as I go in. I sight along the sword toward the one spot, about as big as a dollar and high on the bull's shoulders, where the sword can pass between the blades and honestly kill him. As I come to his head, I reach over to shove in the sword. But at that moment he hooks, and the sword hits bone that feels hard as granite.

His right horn jerks up between my legs, tossing me into the air. Someone tries to help me up, but I am mad, so mad at the stubborn little creature who won't fight or

could lead him. Killing wasn't difficult for me in the first place. I like it, feel most relaxed and confident in killing, but I still have much to learn in that, too. My training in music and art was beneficial to me. Sculpture can be very symbolic, and when you get that in a ring with your own body and bull and cape, it's art. Patience is most necessary, the realization that you have to work at something to make it evolve. It's intangible, but if you work at it hard enough and have genuine desire you'll develop it. It's more spiritual than physical.

For a beginner everything can be a lesson. There isn't much time to think out procedures once the bull is fought. If he is good he won't give you the time, in any case; each part of the body must instinctively cooperate to produce the right maneuver. In my third fight in Juarez, where I was practicing every day, I had tried to modify a pass after the bull had charged and he literally embraced and fell on top of me. I looked up and there he was staring at me, my head out behind his foreleg. His tongue was out, and I felt his hot breath panting in my face. He couldn't reach me, so we just looked at each other until the banderilleros got excited and tried to get him up. We'd have been better off if they'd left us alone, I thought. We'd have got up in time, but he knew where he had me.

On Monday morning, Don Juan Bilbao, of the Juarez ring, arrived at the hotel with Alejandro Montani, who

(continued on page 145)

charge that I push away my helper. I trastear him again, talking to him sharply. I profile and go in again over his horn and this time the sword enters as though into butter and I hunch myself over the lowered horn as he turns away after the cloth. He staggers around a couple of times and falls to his knees. There is an ovation, probably because I have gone in clean a second time after being tossed. I bow to the judge and go behind the barrier to ask Alejandro what I could have done better.

"Don't worry about him, he's dead. He was the worst of the lot. Because of that he was paired with the best — that's your next bull."

"He'd better be the best." I growl.

He was perfect, bless him. I planted my feet and gave him all the muleta passes in my repertoire. I never moved while he charged or passed me. Not once did I have to chase him. I would cite and call out endearingly, for I love the brave bull, and he'd come, close and fast. His horn once ripped my shirt as he tried hooking on the way by. I hated to stop the muleta work, but he was learning so fast that if I kept it up he'd know enough to escape the muleta and take me. Also he was tiring me. I lined him up and killed him to the bedlam of a screaming, shouting audience. I went to the dead bull, who had given me such a chance to prove myself and who was responsible for the good performance, and gave him a few pats on the head. I stoked his nose.

Newspapers printed stories about me that were not always accurate as they were sensational. I was called "the blonde Goddess of the Bullring" until I worried lest the appellation stick.

I was learning, little by little. I discovered that formulas had to be made to fit each bull as he is fought. I had to learn about the lines of fight and whether or not high or low passes were best in each situation; to fight as the bull wished until I had him under control so that I

ARTICULOS
"DANDY"

Hey, Fellas! We've gotten a lot of mail concerning technical advances in women's underthings and especially on how it seems that the male's needs have been grossly neglected. In the name of fairness, we at CAD have decided to reveal some...

BRAS
FOR MEN
by MOTT

Hmm... Let's see. You're in your favorite chair with a tall frosty one, the game's on the tube (with good reception, even!) and you're perusing the latest edition of CAD... Hey ya dope! You forgot the bottle opener! Good thing your gal's got a couple handy, right?!

Ever get tired of the endless search for a pool chalk? Now, they're in a easy-to-keep-track-of spot! Pretend you've got a bead on the cue ball and slam your stick home, bwah!

Say! ...Anybody seen the lighter? Yeh, it's usually buried under cards, half-eaten sandwiches or the winner's chips! This new solution makes sure you always have a lighter at your fingertips!

For the Audiophile: The ultimate high in high fidelity! High grade woofers and tweeters make all the difference! The Bird Man was made to be heard like this!

Go ahead! Take that Mulligan! You've already got a second shot lined up with this new gimmick! 'Playing it as it lies' may be a little more fun now than it used to be!

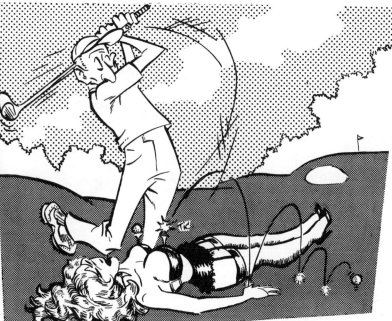

The Swiss Army bra is the perfect companion for that camping trip up north; ...can opener, awl, spoon, screwdrivers, shovel, ball-peen hammer... only, where is that damn fish scaler?!

Burlesque U.S.A.

urlesque is dead. That strangely provocative art form which spawned top banana Phil Silvers, sky-rocketed Gypsy Rose Lee to the status of a national phenomenon, and invented the strip that pleases while it teases, has gone the way of silent movies. The bluenosed puritans who banished it from 42nd Street censored it out of Boston and edged it out Washington, have finally court-ordered it out of Newark and modified it in Union City. It's a quiet, sorry sort of death for a lusty, busty entertainment that couldn't be contained on the stage and had to spill out on a runway. The gentle shuttering of Minsky's and the Hudson caused less clang and clatter that a rhinestone G-string sliding down a polished tuba.

In its heyday, burlesque was synonymous with all that was risque and racy. In the beginning, however, it was a surprisingly prim sort of satirical review. The first hint of nudity came with the introduction of the living-statue bit. It was all on a very high moral and intellectual plane. The shapely young ladies' tableaus resembled classical sculpture groupings. Included were numbers called "The Three Graces," "Adam's First View of Eve," and an ensemble number, with the whole cast on stage, modestly titled "The Rape of the Sabines." Eventually the flesh-colored tights the damsels donned for the occasion gave way to a thin layer of white, or slinky bronze, body paint.

After some initial hollers of horror from the local women's groups, flesh display settled down as a permanent part of burlesque until the ladies of the tableau latched onto a new concept; "free love," that splendid new idea which was sweeping the country. The services of the artistes as "esoteric consultants" were available immediately after each show. Huge billboards outside announced this fact until the gendarmes with an older, simpler name for this same routine put a quash on the whole idea.

To Miss Millie de Leon should go the credit for inventing the first hint of

what was to develop into the strip. This young lady, with a bust-waist-hip ratio that could hardly be matched by any two modern-day fashion models, introduced a brand new twist. Following a momentous build-up, she slowly and ostentatiously removed the garter. After a suitable delay, she delicately tossed this bit of feminine frill to the audience. The mutton-chop and Van Dyke set in the front row promptly clobbered one another to get it. This simple bit of showmanship opened the door to a whole parade of strippers, peelers, fanners, bust bouncers, tassel-twirlers and other *artistes*.

The strip, a stark, brazen exhibition spawned indirectly by Victorian prudishness and nurtured by ankle-length modesty, and above all, so different from the little woman at home, suddenly zoomed to national prominence. When Ann Corio offered a few choice words of advice to a novice stripper, they were breathlessly reported to millions of palpitating readers: "Don't take off your panties," said Miss Corio, "it makes a girl's figure look prettier to have those little gadgets on."

Ann Corio did far more. She gave a permanent, almost classic form to "look but don't touch" — the "flash"

or entrance in full costume, the "parade" or long-legged strut across the stage, the "tease" or gradual shedding and finally the "pose" in glimmering skin and G-string just before the black-out. Credit for the ritualistic bumps and grinds, unfortunately, has been lost in obscurity.

And it was fun, too. The time was ripe for a fad, and the strip flourished. Gypsy Rose Lee gave it a new twist. She added patter composed equally of intellectual fluff and double entendre which she would recite while working the ramp. Patter went further than peeling, for Gypsy stopped far short of the show-it-all girls. Her finale featured two quivering petals and a fair-sized bow. Another runway pioneer was Rose La Rose, who set a new standard for stamina. Her record for bumps-per-minute has never been beaten, equaled or even approached. Hers was a dazzling brand of performance, which played havoc with the overworked pit drummer and scorched the plush upholstery in the first four rows of seats.

Then there was Sally Keith, who introduced tassels — one to a breast. They whirled clockwise, counter-clockwise, together, opposed and individually. The act was later expanded

to include similar effect to the rear.

Another great innovator, Carrie Fennell, quivered everything. She would start a shimmy down around her ankles and let it roll slowly upward, gathering momentum until it culminated in an incredible degree of mammary vibration. Carrie in motion, was an unforgettable sight. Never a slender willow, she has since assumed hefty proportions, but her ample endowments still jiggle and romp with the old-time abandon.

The darling of Manhattan's Lower East Side, in burlesque's heyday, was a rather ordinary peeler with an extraordinary name. When "Rosie Tookus" went up in lights on a Jersey marquee, Second Avenue made a mass exodus to Newark.

The standard item of final apparel, the G-string, took on new sparkle and glitter as the strippers struggled for individuality. With matte-black, spangle-covered, rhinestone-covered and fringed "G's" becoming quite common, Carmen Bridges brought a fresh, new idea to the runway. Her G-string contained a little electric bulb which made a nifty effect as it winked coyly through the plumage of her fans. (There was considerable debate at the time concerning the concealment of the batteries.)

Other stars quickly shot into prominence. Sherry Britton made a prim and proper entrance, then shed her air of aloof refinement with the first zipper. Margie Hart worked down to a fishnet dress. Georgia Southern frequently prefaced with a ditty of her own composition but swiftly got to the serious action of tearing down the curtains. Lili St. Cyr blended art with rhinestone pasties while Evelyn Mayers, Jeanne Carrol, Betty Howland and Gladys Clark built up a loyal following, each using their own unique charms and techniques.

As the flood of strippers assumed gigantic proportions, Countess Nadja and Hinda Wassau each developed an exotic, off-beat routine to go with their names. Jeanne Adair, "The Mystery Girl" removed her sequined mask only after doffing her bra. Lois De

Fee banked on a massive frame to lift her out of the ordinary. When she bumped, over six feet of well-stacked female bumped. And a grind carried the momentum of a piledriver. When an eclipse threatened her career, she married a midget and started over on a new crest of publicity.

Princess La Homa laid claim to full-blooded Choctaw ancestry along with her title, and sported a full-length feather headdress to prove it. And a nice contrast it made, too, behind a full expanse of skin just before the spotlight winked out. Scarlet Kelly, on the other hand, made full use of a waist-length hank of flaming hair that highlighted her frenzied action.

Then came the animal parade. When Rosita

Royce switched from a routine strip to an act with a covy of ambitious doves who plucked her naked for the quota of birdseed, she unleashed a flood of imitators. Any furred or feathered beast who could be trained to tug at a zipper and not disgrace himself on stage found ready employment. These little helpers ranged from a macaw to Sally Lane's Capuchin monkey.

The final fillip was a shift to trick names. Certainly Ann Tenna, Peppy Cola and Jan Tiffany ("The Jewel of Broadway") are names to conjure with. But Alky Seltzer ("The Bumps and Burps Girl") can't be readily forgotten nor Bonnie Bell ("The Ding Dong Girl"), for that matter. Ginger ("Wham-Wham") Jones lived up to her billing and Patti Wagon added an earthy touch.

The girls of burlesque followed a stylized form in their routines, and the comics were equally classic. Their humor was at the opposite pole from the current anemia of television with its ability to devour comedians and material at a frightening clip. Skits? There were no skits. Not really. There were bits. Hand a burley comic a gavel and he could go off into anyone of fifty courtroom bits. "Order in the court!" "Yes, your whoreship." Roll out the bar set and he was ready for drinking bits ad infinitum. The doctor's office? He reached for that mammoth hypodermic. "Oh, Doctor, I'm so nervous." "Well, stop squirming. How do you expect me to get my needle in!" Ditto for the street corner, the bedroom, the firehouse, etc.

The humor was bawdy and rowdy, with a frank acceptance of sex that bordered on the obscene. But the time-worn bits, despite blank pistols and seltzer bottles, had the easy, comfortable familiarity of an old friend. To the burlesque aficionado, anticipating the gags was part of the fun.

Make-up and costume for the comic was standard. If it wasn't a red putty nose and loose-ly-anchored baggy pants with the crotch drooping down to around the knees, it was a bald wig, jacket with palm-sized plaid and a necktie ending at ankles. The get-up, plus a handful of stock wheezes, identified each man. The "Ga, Ga, Ga" of Bert Lahr was as much a part of him as his race-track suits. Billy Hagan wasn't really on stage until the first "Cheeeeeeese 'n Crackers." Sam Howe had "Oh, that's my horse," and could shoehorn it into an amazing number of situations. And during moments of extreme stress, or upon being goosed, Dave Marion's half-strangulated aside of

Dancing to the beat of a bongo drummer, Betty Howard is a truly torrid performer.

ell, I'm a sonofa bitch," carried to the top balcony.

What's become of the comics of burlesque — the top bananas and the aight men? Pick a channel from 1 to 13. The putty noses were left behind a trunk in Detroit, but they are still dispensing the same brand of humor. eir "new" gags are just cleaned-up "blue" jokes.

Phil Silvers is far better known today for his Sergeant Bilko than he ever s for his burley routines. Jackie Gleason and his multi-million dollar TV ntract are, of course, legendary. Leon Errol continued his rubber-legged lk into Hollywood, Bobby Clark shifted to films and the legit stage. For bott and Costello it was radio, then films. Ditto Fanny Brice and Jack arl.

The burlesque wheels — Columbia, Empire, Mutual, and the rest who e sent scores of shows trooping the country — have closed shop. Noth- remains but the tired, ragged remnants of a once great medium. The few rley houses left, totter along, squeezed between dwindling receipts and gety censors.

The era of burlesque is over. It is finished and through and dead.

But it's good to remember when.

— *Walt Fishman*

by Doug Bonde

The only real difference between a prize-fighter and a stripper is that they have their muscles in different places. That sums up near-ly everything important about the subject, and I ought to know. I'm the lucky guy who spent 15 years training fighters and suddenly found him-self training strippers instead.

A lot of people think that a switch like mine, from the ring to the runway, is about on a par with a leopard changing his spots — impos-sible. They don't understand what a guy who's spent most of his life putting pugs through their paces with sparring partners and punching bags in a smelly gym could possibly have to teach a lissome lovely about the ins and outs of theatri-cal semi-seduction. In fact, a good many of them think it's pretty funny. Well, they're wrong.

Actually, training a stripper and training a fighter are very similar occupations, though if you ask me, there is no difficulty in choosing

THE FINE ART

between them. I'll take the strippers every day, even if the work is harder.

And it is harder, believe me. Many of my old cronies, and a lot of laymen, too, envy me because they see only the glamour side of my job, and of course there is no denying that the glamour helps make up for the grief.

But handling a stripper is like handling a wildcat — temperament, women's intuition, and the well-known wiles of the so-called "weaker sex" make a gal a much trickier propo-sition to boss around than a fighter who relies on you to plan his every move. Often, a gal will agree to go along with an idea you have, then do exactly what she intended to in the beginning. And if you bawl her out for it, she cries or throws things. Fighters don't behave that way, even when they break training.

All this pays off, however, when you come up with a champion, just as all the long hours of hard work with a fighter pay off with a win-ning boy.

DO-MAY, part-Cherokee, part-Irish newcomer to burlesque appears in dress of Indian forbears. She hails from Nevada and has been favorite in Las Vegas with performance which includes totem pole and consists of slowly discarding feathers.

As an example, let me offer the case of Do-May, "The Cherokee Half-Breed," champion in my stable of strippers and an Indian princess who is really making the braves in night clubs all over the country sit up and take notice. When I first saw Do-May in a Louisville, Kentucky, club, she wasn't known as Do-May. She was a pretty girl with some really outstanding attributes, and a lot of energy but absolutely no polish. I thought I could do something for her, and I told her so. As a matter of fact, I married her, but that came later and is part of our private, not professional, lives.

I feel that strippers, like fighters, are born, not made. They have to have a natural instinct. By that I mean they must know, without thinking, how to "tease" and when to do it. They have to be gifted with sexy facial expresssions, and these are created only by the inner impulse. Some girls might be beautiful, but they could never look sexy if they were to try all day. On the other hand, the girl with the natural instinct can't look anything else but sexy, even in G.I. boots and fatigue clothes.

Of course a well-rounded figure and especially a large bust are musts for top strippers today, because of the tastes of the public. But here is where training and polish come in, for these can be built, and the girl with the natural instinct can be made into a shining star of the night club stage by skillful emphasis

OF TRAINING STRIPPERS

of her best parts.

Do-May, however, had "outstanding" qualifications in every way. She tapes in at a neat 39-24-36, and once prompted Milton Berle to remark, "Do-May has the kind of shape the world should be in." I'll agree.

Even so, there was a lot of work yet to be done. Do-May had a lot, but she didn't know how to use it. As soon as she signed with me, I set up a training schedule designed to correct this. Here once again is a similarity with my former work with fighters. Men have certain muscles they develop to give them the "body beautiful" and so do women, if they would only take the time to develop them.

Don't get me wrong. I don't mean a girl should look like Mr. America, but she can develop the hidden muscles that bring out her most feminine attributes. The majority of women have beautiful bodies if they would only take care of them. If they spent one half the time on their bodies as they do on their hair and faces, the manufacturers of built-in "bazooms" would be out of business.

That isn't the only virtue of exercise, however. Every muscle in a woman's body can be used to great advantage on the

(continued on page 142)

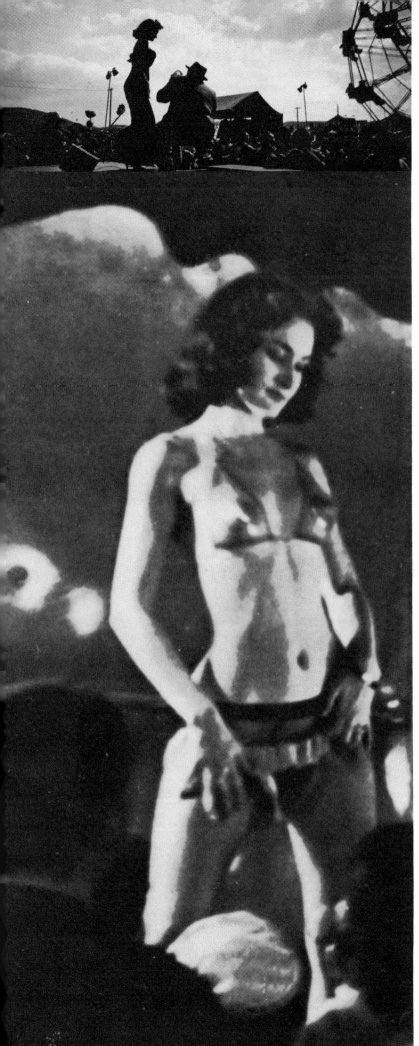

by Milton Machlin

Girls! Girls! Girls! Step a little closer folks, the girls won't bite you, on the other hand, don't you bite them. That girl with the stars in her eyes is little Aspasia from Asia, and when you see her dance inside, I guarantee you're going to say "No wonder your little Aspasia." I hold up my hand and what do you see, men? Skin! Well, I'm not lyin' when I tell you that's just what you're going to see on the inside. You little ladies that are watching — you might step in and see what it takes to interest a man. If you're not broadminded — well, the merry-go-round is right down the midway. You married folks step in too, you might learn something. When this girl comes out again she's going to be wearing nothing but three gardenias: one here, one here, and one right where you're now looking buddy. The box office is open now and the show goes on in just three minutes. Only the first fifty customers can be admitted. Don't block the ticket stand, folks, let 'em get in and buy their tickets ...

Show me a man who hasn't been a mark for the girl-show barker's spiel at least once in his life, and I'll show you a man who doesn't eat his Wheaties. Despite the fact that most men have seen more of the glittergals than they have of their own wives and sweethearts, there is less known about the behind-the-scenes operation of a girl show than is probably known about any other branch of show (and I do mean "show") business.

Where do the girls who parade their talcumed torsos on midways from Surf Avenue in Coney Island to the Sacramento State Fair come from? Are they good girls or bad girls? What do they do when they're not peeling for the marks? How far do they go? What happens in those little shows that you pay extra for after the main event?

Where do they come from? The fact is, says veteran girl-show operator Frank Garto, "that the carnival or Coney Island-type girl show is one of the best places for a dame to bust into show business. We're almost always shorthanded when it comes to good-looking bimbos. Even with the girls the different agents send me, I hardly ever have enough. I have to scout around a lot on my own. We get all kinds of girls —former waitresses, dance hall hostesses hustlers too, once in a while, but not often. A good hustler can make too much dough on the outside. We got three kinds of girls working in the shows. The ones who 'ride the white horse' — the stars, so to speak; they can pull down the good money if they're real name attractions. The regular line girls who work on the bally — that's the platform in front where we give out the free samples and do a little shake routine inside, pick up some decent change. Then there's the filler-pigs. These are some broads who aren't such great lookers or who just can sex it up enough to keep the customers happy. They get maybe a hundred simoleons a week, and lucky to get it."

A good girl-show worker, Frank believes, is born, not made. "Some of these broads just love to get up there and tease — I think they like it better than the real thing." Many of them don't realize the tantalizing power of a beautiful body until they've worked a while in a show.

One girl Garto hired for the Danbury Fair midway had never worked a girl show in her life. But she was a good looking "head" with a set of thirty eights that were worth their lively weight in

Bally Girls

admission tickets, so Garto showed her a few simple dance steps and asked her to get up and work the bally for a while till she got the feel of things. "She was a shy kid, kind of scared, and we practically had to wrassle her into her costume the first night. We couldn't find a bra in the joint to fit her so we had to improvise one at the last minute from a cheesecloth mosquito-net. It looked good, too, with a couple sequins sewn on it here and there."

The first night the girl was so scared that she had to bolster herself with a couple of slugs in order to get up the nerve to face the marks who were clustered out front like overripe grapes ready for the picking. The liquor seemed to help, and the second night she was much more at ease — with the help of about six slugs of the happy sauce. By the end of the week the barker was referring to her as "our Miss Carstairs." But the marks loved her, and she began to have an awareness of the beauty of her own body that had never penetrated her dim consciousness before.

"She was coining dough for us," Garto reminisces sadly, "but I had to drop her. One night I'm standing near the ticket box counting the take when I hear the marks making such a rumpus in the tent I thought it was a 'rube' (fight). I look inside, and what do I see? Miss Carstairs is stripped to her daget (G-string in carny lingo) and she's getting ready to jump out of that. I reach for the switch and throw out every light in the joint while I hustle her off the stage. The marks are sore as hell but I cool them out, and finally get the tent empty without having it torn down around me. 'Baby,' I says, 'what do you think you are doing? You know we don't allow no strip here. You want to get us all pinched? You want to lose me my license?'"

The girl was sulky. "Gee whiz!" she mumbled, nearly flooring Garto with her 90-proof breath. "You told me to get sexy."

From that time on there was no way of holding down Miss Carstairs. She had the old exhibitionist fever. She loved to be loved, and where else could she get 50 men at once drooling over her beauty? Every time Garto turned around the blonde bombshell was trying to give the marks more than they paid for.

"I finally had to dump her," Garto said regretfully. "It was self-defense."

Once, when Garto had two girls working for him, a blonde and a brunette, there was a fight which is still classic in girl-show history. The dark haired one was called Princess Anne, and the blonde, whose long silky hair was almost her entire costume, was known as Godiva. One midsummer night, when heat and a full moon had raised temperatures to a fever pitch, the Princess Anne got her mitts into Godiva's hair, it was curtains for that lady. There was a ripping sound, like that of a band-aid parting from skin, and the shapely Princess found herself with a handful of fragrant fluff that had once been Godiva's crowning glory. Godiva's hair had been a wig! A hush fell on the fellow troupers who had gathered to see the fight, and Princess Anne was so flustered that she stopped fighting, and blushing for the first time in her life, handed the wig back to Godiva who lay face down on the floor with her hands clutched over her head, too embarrassed to even get to her knees. By mutual consent the crowd departed leaving Godiva to her shame. Did she leave the show?

"No," says Garto, "she was a trouper. She finished out the season and nobody never let on that they seen nothing. Funny thing is that from then on, her and the Princess were like bosom buddies, if you know what I mean."

Jack Dadswell, an oldtime carnival press agent describes an incident involving another Godiva, in his book *Hey There, Sucker!*

This Godiva had a front piece of truly Texan proportions. A well-dressed customer who was surveying the scene turned to Dadswell and asked:

"Are those real?"

Dadswell assured him that they were.

"Ah-h-h," the customer sighed deeply, "would that I were a millionaire."

"What would you do if you were a millionaire, my friend?" Dadswell asked.

"If I were a millionaire," the customer continued dreamily, "I'd buy six acres of those things and walk around barefooted."

The sight of a girl-show lovely has inspired many a mark to similar dreams. It is these dreams that turn to gold for the girl-show operators who cash in on the trance-like state induced by the soft lights and sweet curves inside the show tent by means of a "blow-off." A blow-off is carny talk for an extra show for which additional money is paid once the customer is in the tent. You've all heard the spiel:

"And now folks, for those of you who like a little extra spice with your meals, I don't have to tell you that we are limited by the law as to what we can show the general public. But if you will give the gentleman at the rear flap an additional fifty cents to pay for the extra electricity, I think we can show you what you've been talking about in the back rooms of the barber shops and in locker rooms all year while you were waiting for the carnival to come to town..."

The law does proscribe what can be shown, and for that reason it is seldom in most parts of the country that the customer gets to see anything but a reworked version of what he has just finished looking at. This is known in the trade as a "rehash."

But in some sections of the country, such as the mining towns of Tennesseee, Pennsylvania and Kentucky, the paying customers are tougher and the law less vigilant, and in these places the real "Cootch" show operates — where, as the barker says, "everything goes when the whistle blows." This is also true in the rural sections of the deep south. In some shows the customers are even permitted to step up and handle the merchandise if they are in any doubts as to its reality.

More usual than the cootch show, which is the roughest kind, are the "Mediokus" shows such as Garto operates. These are shows which depend on good-looking and scantily dressed girls who can quiver and quake in the classic vein to accompaniment of a rhumba, a cha-cha-cha or a rock 'n roll beat. These are not exactly shows you would take your Aunt from Winona to, at least not most old aunts, but they aren't hot enough to get the owner or the girls pinched for indecency either.

Strip-teasers are never permitted in the Mediokus shows. Generally the girl comes out in a fairly scanty garment to start with, takes off one

or two wisps, and finishes her act in either a bra and G-string, or pasties, which are little clusters of sequins about the size of a silver dollar and serve to cover the bulls-eye area of the bosom enough to satisfy the letter of the law.

Least satisfying of all are known — for obvious reasons — as Sunday School shows. In general these shows dominate the midway of the big traveling carnivals like the James Straits shows, the World of Mirth, and the more elaborate state fairs.

"It ain't like it used to be," Garto says. "You can't work strong any more." But still the marks come in. And the call of the barker still lights a fire in most men. One overexcited mark nearly got Garto in trouble last season. Garto was stacking quarters for his trip to the bank when a plainclothesman from the local Coney Island precinct dropped in for a chat.

"Had a complaint," the cop remarked casually. "Man says the manager of this here show clipped him for fifty bucks."

Frank, who is strictly a showman and has never attempted to con game, was flabbergasted.

"A cannon?" he asked, inquiring whether the man had been the victim of a pickpocket.

"Nope," the cop said, cleaning his nails with his badge, "this man says that when Za-Za was up there shaking it, the manager of this here show comes along and offered to fix up a private date with her after the show. The guy took a fifty buck deposit on the merchandise and disappeared into the tent. Never showed up again. The complainant says that when he tried to claim Za-Za, you fellas wouldn't turn her over to him. What do you say to that?" The cop asked the question with a straight face, so Garto answered straight.

"What did this man look like, that called himself the manager?"

"He was tall and thin, and had red hair."

Garto, who is five feet four in heavy stockings and measures slightly less than that from side to side, indicated his balding pate.

"Well, I ain't no redhead," he observed.

The cop looked at him. "No, I guess you're not," he said.

"My guess," Garto said, "is that this red-headed guy bought himself a ticket in advance, cased the mark, gave him the pitch, took the moolah, and bugged out through the back door while the mark was standing there with egg on his face waiting."

Garto laughed at the memory of it. "Them marks, you can never tell what they're gonna do. I'll never forget the time at the Minelo Fair when one of them bounced a Long Island potato off my cruller because the show wasn't hot enough."

What about the show he has on the Coney Island midway now? Is that hot enough?

"Well, you know, down in that tropical climate like they got down there in Hawaii it ain't natural to overload yourself with no extra clothing. You step inside and I guarantee you, you're gonna see something that will make you know where we got our theme song."

Which is?

"She's got the biggest Kanakas in Hawaii."

And why do the marks like you and me, and him over there, keep coming back year after year after year?

"It's alive, it moves. It's warm, it shakes. You don't get nothing like that on a tv screen, Jack."

That's Garto's theory and he sticks to it. Turning from us he pokes his head behind the flap and shouts at his cast of characters.

"Okay girls, Bally! Bally! Get out there and shake it."

WARD IN ITALY

I was happy to discover that derriere-pinching
in Rome had not gone out of style.

WARD IN HAWAII

The tropical climate and customs here made
for unusual behavior patterns.

WARD'S DREAM WORLD

MOST globe-trotters need passports, air sickness pills and their international Diners' Club card before they can get to those booze- and broad-happy bacchanals known in the travel folders as foreign ports of call. Not Bill Ward — he needs only his sketchbook, his pencil, and his lively imagination. Too busy with the prosaic tasks of making his daily bread by cartooning, commercial art and other similar endeavors heaped on a much-in-demand artist, Ward has never had the opportunity to loll in the tropical sunshine or schuss down an Alp slope. So, he does the next best thing, he draws himself visiting exotic places, happily inhabited by truly exotic women. It is as if Ward uses his pencil as a magic wand; just a wave of it and "voila," he's in Italy, Hawaii, Turkey, et al. Obviously, swingin' foreign chicks are what make Ward's dream world go 'round — laughing all the way. So dream and laugh along now with Bill Ward on these next pages.

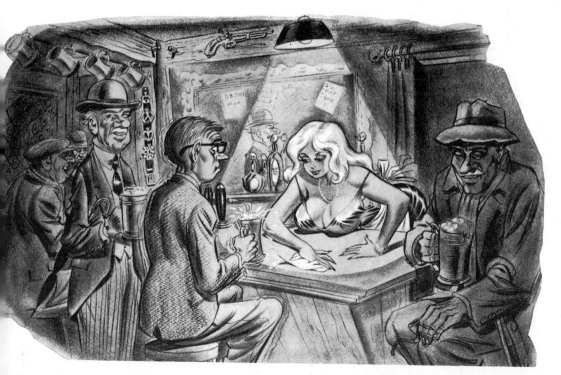

WARD IN ENGLAND

I was rather shocked to find not all English girls were tweedy or flat-chested.

WARD'S DREAM WORLD

WARD IN SPAIN

My 'moment of truth' came from the grandstand, not the arena.

WARD IN JAPAN

I was determined to find more to do in Japan than just bathing.

WARD IN SWEDEN

I found the
Suana baths to be more
invigorating then
I had ever imagined.

WARD IN FRANCE

Contrary to popular opinion, American credit cards
are not always accepted for services rendered.

WARD IN ARABIA

I quickly realized that exotic entertainment abroad
could be had on a modest expense account.

Dr. Voronoff and the Monkey Gland Transplants

by Adam Parfrey

It is said of daring and virile men that they've "got balls." Rarely has a cliché bared such a fundamental truth of Nature. For without two healthy sex glands hanging in his hairy scrotal pouch, a man could hardly be called ... a man.

Dr. Serge Voronoff, prophet of the gland-grafting rejuvenators Patrick McGrady has called "The Erector Set," served early in his career as attending physician to the eunuchs of Khedive Abbas II's harem. Voronoff made the first-hand discovery that the ball-less lost more than just the ability to have children. Beyond the baleful side-effects of corpulence and a lack of *joie de vivre*, few of the eunuchs lived past the age of 60.

Doc Voronoff came to realize the secret to a man's power and long life was to be found in his *cojones*. A fundamental law of animal husbandry was finally applied to mankind. Any 4-H member can tell you that a lazy, fat capon is produced by castrating a bellicose rooster. Geld a belligerent bull and you've created a placid, agreeable oxen. Reverse the process, Voronoff hypothesized, and it's possible to breathe orgastic potential into the impotent and listless. He began his experiments borrowing the "interstitial glands" of a young and lively ram and grafting them to the sex glands of aged sheep. The results were nothing short of miraculous:

> The horns start growing again, becoming unusually large; the excess fat disappears, the muscles develop, the bodily vigor becomes evident at the most cursory glance. The animals again become aggressive and bellicose, and again seek the females which, evidently comprehending that they possess masculine attributes, display complacent attitudes.

The good doctor was anxious to apply his findings to men. All the way from his Italian chateau, Voronoff had heard news of the stirring experiments of the old sawbones at San Quentin prison in the United States. Dr. Leo L. Stanley was granted permission to rescue "perfectly good" body parts from those who hung from the penitentiary's "gallow of the 13 steps" and transfer those parts to his quite captive patients. In his memoir, *Men at Their Worst*, Stanley recalls the first such operation, hacking off the considerable gonads of a freshly-executed "young negro" and transferring them via surgery to a senile prisoner 72 years of age:

> Patient since his operation has improved mentally and physically. His eyes are brighter and he is more active mentally and physically than a man many years his junior. Appetite is excellent. He is anxious to be about doing something of interest. Before operation he was naturally reticent, but now is positively emphatic ... An odd result was that for the first time I found him able to comprehend jokes.

Encouraged by this success, Stanley went on to carry out hundreds of human testes transplants, and because "the amount of human material was limited," Stanley began to sew ram balls on all those prisoners who desired their testosterone kick, or time off for good behavior under the blade. Voronoff was envious of Dr. Stanley's pre-Mengele laboratory well-stocked with human glands and organs. But unlike Stanley, Voronoff had no supply of live young homo sapiens' testes for his doddering rejuvenees, and was forced to search the wild kingdom for a species whose nuts were sympathetic to human transplant. "Fortunately," wrote Voronoff, "we have in the animal world a close relative from whom we can make such a loan with a minimum of scruples: orangutans, chimpanzees, gibbons."

"The greatest monkey hunt of all time was on. From the equatorial forests of central and west Africa, hunters white and black began ensnaring the outraged anthropoids by the hundreds and shipping them across the Mediterranean to Voronoff's vast, hillside *singerie* below the majestic Chateau Grimaldi, on the outskirts of Ventimiglia on the Italian Rivera." (McGrady, *The Youth Doctors*.)

The monkey business had begun in earnest. To Voronoff's retreat the very rich went, often to choose the particular chimp whose spry set of testes were to gift those who could afford the expensive gland transplant operation with an invigorated and perhaps enlongated life.

The technique of the Voronoff gland transplant was simple. He would remove the huevos of the donor monkey, slicing the gland into six parts. These six fragments would then be stitched directly to the surface capillaries of the recipient's own testis. Dr. Voronoff recalls his first success in the human sphere, the sight of his rejuvenated patient, who once appeared so droopy and lifeless and now stood before him like a man reborn, erect and alert. Overcome with emotion, Voronoff was certain of his conquest over Nature: "I saw realized before me the legend of Faust without the subject having had need to sell his soul to the devil."

Voronoff the romantic, who lamented the cruelty of time and physical deterioration on the human spirit, imagined that he had evaded giving the devil his due. But beyond his chauvinism about the value of a senile human life being greater than a monkey's, Voronoff was mistaken about realizing the legend of Faust — for the Russian doctor possessed a greater resemblance to Count Dracula. In the Voronoffian operation the life-giving substance is hacked from one animal to empower another. Voronoff had not "found" a secret of vitality so much as discovered a method of transferrence. Whoever could afford Voronoff's operation would endow himself with the life-force of animals conveniently lower in the food chain. The principle was employed by the medieval monster Elizabeth Bathory; by bathing in the blood of slaughtered maidservants she protected her skin against aging.

Voronoff declared that he had successfully subdued Nature. But ultimately he could not subdue public opinion. A cabal of anti-vivesectionists sided with more conventionally-minded gerontologists to vilify Voronoff's work. Scientists held Voronoff's surgical techniques up to ridicule, claiming that human testes would almost immediately "reject" such foreign material as a monkey gland. The claims of Voronoff's published papers were scoffed at due to the lack of appropriate statistical procedures, such as the use of control groups. Though improvements were noted in the health and mental condition of many human and animal graftees, very few scientists beside Voronoff were willing to attribute their renewed well-being to gland transplantation.

The public was largely incredulous at the notion of the marriage of human and simian sex glands, especially in the shadow of the Scopes trial. Caricatures of Voronoff appeared in popular literature and in the movies, usually bathetic melodramas in which a mad scientist would transform an upstanding citizen into a Mr. Hyde, with all the attendant tragic circumstances. Despite the scorn, the independently wealthy Voronoff radicalized his views. He suggested to a conference in Budapest in 1927 that bright children should be gland-grafted early in life to be endowed with even greater powers. "I call," said Voronoff, "for children of genius. Give me such children, and I will create a new super-race of men of genius."

By the 1930s, Voronoff's reputation diminished further. The vulgar began to associate the great Voronoff with the notorious Dr. John Brinkley whose farm of Toggenburg goats provided the glands for all those with $750 in hand for the transplantation operation. Brinkley's gland operations revived the Texas town of Del Rio and powered the million watt Border Radio station XERA.

Gland transplants began to give way to a new sort of rejuvenation treatment, Dr. Paul Niehans' vaunted technique of cell therapy. Rather than transplanting gonads, the Swiss genius would mash and liquify the glands for subcutaneous injection via an intimidatingly large horse needle. Niehans' greatest hour of triumph came in 1953, when he was summoned to the bedside of Pope Pius XII, then at the brink of death. Niehans brought in two pregnant ewes to the Vatican and had them

"Is gland-daughter proud of her gland-papa?"

A TRIUMPH for SCIENCE!

(continued on page 143)

Those weren't monkey glands you sold me!

CEASE ROOD *BOAROUS* CLUSTRING RAILER
LISTEN YOU LANDSMEN *ALL* TO ME
MESSMATES HERE A *BROTHER SAILOR*
SING THE *DANGERS* OF THE SEAS
FROM BOWLING BILLOWS FIRST IN MOTION
TO THE TEMPAST TROUBLED *OCEAN*
WHEN THE DISTANT *WHIRLWIND* RAISE
WHEN THE *SEAS* CONTEND WITH *SKIES*

HARK THE *BOATSWAIN* LOUDLY BALING
BY TOP SAIL GALLANTS QUICK BE HALLING
DOWN TOP SHEETS AND HALYARDS *STAND*
DOWN YOUR STAY SAILS HAND BOYS HAND
NOW IT *FRESHENS* SET THE BRACES
THE *LEE* TOP SAIL SHEETS LET GO
LOUFF BOYS LUFF DON'T MAKE *RYE* FACES
UP YOUR TOP SAILS NIMBLY *CLEW*

126

NOW TO ALL YOU IN DOWN BEDS *SPORTING*
FONDLY *LOCKED* IN BEAUTIES ARMS
FRESH ENJOYMENTS WANTON COURTING
FREE FROM ALL BUT *LOVES* ALARMS
ROUND US ROARS THE *TEMPEST* LOUDER
HARK YE HOW WHAT *FEAR* INTHRAWLS
HARDER YET IT YET BLOWS HARDER
NOW AGAIN THE *BOATSWAIN'S* CALL

YOUR TOP SAIL YARDS POINT TO THE *WIND* BOYS
SEE ALL CLEAR TO REACH EACH COURSE
LET YOUR *FORESHEET* GO DON'T MIND BOYS
THOUGH THE WEATHER SHOULD BE *WORSE*
FORE AND AFT YOUR SPRITE SAIL YARD GETT
REEF YOUR *MIZZEN* SEE ALL CLEAR
HANDS AT EACH PROVENTOR BRACE SETT
MAN THE FORE YARD CHEAR LADS CHEAR

NOW THE *DREADFUL* THUNDER RATTLES
PEEL ON PEAL CONTENDING *CLASH*
ON OUR HEADS *FEARS* RAIN FALL POWERING
IN OUR EYES BLEW LIGHTNING FLASH
ONE WIDE WATER ALL AROUND US
ALL ABOVE US ONE *BLACK SKYE*
DIFFERENT DEATHS AT ONCE SURROUND US
HARK WHAT MEANS THE DREADFUL *CRYE*

THE FORE MAST'S *GONE* CRYS EVERY TONGUE OUT
OVER THE LEE 12 FEET ABOVE THE DECK
A *LEAK* BENEATH THE CHESTREES SPRUNG OUT
CALL ALL HANDS TO CLEAR THE WRECK
QUICK THE LANYARDS *CUT* TO PIECES
COME MY HEARTS BE *STOUT* AND BOLD
PLUMB THE WILL THE LEAK *INCREASES*
FOUR FEETE WATER IN THE *HOLE*

Ask the D.I.

DEAR D.I.: My wife, Velma, allows me one-half hour a night to relax and read my back issues of CAD and then it's back to dusting and waxing. I barely have time to catch my breath, and then I am forced to orally satisfy Velma for several hours at a time. My question, D.I., is this: How can I tell Velma to wash her privates so that I may not gag at my connubial obligation?

Barney Phyfe
Gay Head, MA

20 ON THE FLOOR, PHYFE, RIGHT NOW!: Ain't no shame in there bein' a little tang to yer poon. Since old Velma Rottencrotch seems to be the pitcher on yer home team, seems to me splashin' a little whisky on her love muffin'l be about the only relief a sorry piece o' shit like you deserves. I've been in the Corps for a good thirty years now, and the one thing I have learned is that men are made, not born, and likewise a man can be un-made. Face it, Barney, you sad sack of shit, any lily-livered coward who lets a woman boss him around ain't fit to read a fine publication like CAD. Leave that to the real men in the world, something that a spineless lap-licking turd such as yourself can never have any hope of being.

DEAR D.I.: What do you think about women who wear pants?

Frank Waldrop
Truth or Consequences, NM

NOW HEAR THIS, WALDROP: If the good lord had intended for women to wear pants, he wouldn't've put the zipper on the backside. I seem to recall the name for the type of women who dress up in men's clothing, and it ain't sweetheart.

DEAR D.I.: I'm no queer, but I'm looking for a square-jawed, hairy-fingered goon to root through some unexplored chamber of my gut with his savage appurtenance. Will you oblige me?

Dick Bender
Washington D.C.

CHRIST ON A FUCKIN' CRUTCH, BENDER: When I opened your letter, I'd noticed the return address and thought that finally I'd gotten a question from a red-blooded American man proud to call our great nation's capitol home. Well, let me tell you, Richard my boy, the only appurtenance you'd find this old soldier probing your sorry faggot ass with would be ten inches of cold blue steel strapped onto the end of my trusty carbine, Mae Belle. It sickens my red, white and blue heart to think that some pinko gook homo should be staining the sacred soil of my beloved capitol when his guts ought to be spread out over a square acre or two of some heathen ay-rab desert terrain. In short, my advice to you, girlie, is to put a quick end to your pathetic, ballet-lovin' life. There just ain't room in my America for the likes of you.

DEAR D.I.: My daughter is running around with some lazy, no-account hippie type, and I'm pig-biting mad. How do I prevent this unholy union?

Rev. Lyle Lemon
Nashville, TN

WELL PADRE: Let's set back a moment and give this a little brainwork before you sink your dentures into Porky. Seems I recall that the main activity of a hippie after a good cluster-fuck and dope-orgy is gimping down and sucking the blood of every tax-payin' American at the local welfare office. So, Rev., let's you and I make a little deal. Next Tuesday, when Mr. Far-Out is standing in line with the rest of the scum, all ya gotta do is slip him some barefoot boy's version of a Mickey Finn, and once you got that hop-head seeing stars, point him in the direction of the nearest recruiting office for Semper Fi. You can bet your bible that once I get my hands on Mr. Long-Hair, he'll be too busy prying my boot-tip out of his unwashed mother-lovin' ass to be giving your flesh and blood the old tube-snake ever again.

by Terry Hammonds

There I was, my back against the wall, alone against a 250 pound psychopath, coming at me with this bone-crusher shank. All I had was my fists, and my skinny 150 pound body.

He was the "shot caller" of our dorm, and he came at me bellowing that nobody crossed him, like I had just done. He planned to "break me off, something terrible," I could tell.

"I don't give a fuck who you think you are. You're just another one of the busters to me," I yelled back at him. "Come on," I continued, grabbing a nearby mop-wringer. "I ain't goin' out like no sucker, specially over just because I changed channels on the tv." Seeing me holding that mop wringer slowed him down; in fact, he stopped coming at me. Now he had to jockey around like a boxer looking for an opening. He suddenly realized that he could get hurt here too.

Like I was to learn later, a lot of these guys became shot callers, not because of their actions, but because of their size, and the actions people thought they might take. Usually most of the doings were done by henchmen, usually a gang of 'em. Alone, guys didn't stand much of a chance unless he bypassed those busters by going "head up" with the shot-caller himself.

He slashed out at me, he missed, and I followed the motion of his hand, cracking it, causing him to drop the shank. When I pulled back to swing again and take him out, one of his boys kicked the shank back over to him. I busted that guy one over the kneecaps for his trouble. I shouldn't have, though, because that gave the shot caller a chance to pick the shank back up. Damn, I thought his boys were going to stay out of this. My only chance was to make enough noise, so that the C.O.s would come and see what was going on in this bathroom, and break it up. "Come on, Motherfuckers!" I screamed.

You know it's weird the shit you think of sometimes. Right then, instead of fear of death going through my head, all I could think was, how the fuck did I come to wind up in this prison bathroom fighting a giant killer?

What the fuck was going through my mind when I stole a lousy three hundred bucks from the college bookstore where I worked? Especially when somebody else was already stealing from there, and I knew I would get blamed for all of it if I got caught. Starving student? Sure, but I could have made it. I didn't have to steal. I guess I'd learned my lesson, but that wasn't going to save me. The things I'd learned growing up on the South Side of town was what was going to help me now.

I could hear the loud slaps of the feet of the police running to the bathroom, then the shouting. "What's going on here? Inmates! Get on your bunks!" I put the mop wringer down, after the shot-caller handed his shank away into the fast dispersing crowd. We both went out together, so as not to let the police have two definite people to suspect of a confrontation, in case someone got to one of us, which I knew would happen, if had to, that's how prison life works. One thing for sure, I decided it wasn't going to be me. I was going to have to do something before lights out tonight. I wasn't going to be one of those people who went to sleep and never woke up. That happens a lot here.

Well, I was originally going to do the thirteen months or a two year sentence here, but now I'm doing life. I'll have done seventeen years by the time I get out now. I'm alive now, which is more than that shot-caller can say.

Sometimes, sitting in my cell in the afternoons, when the sun shines through the window down onto my bunk and my face, I wonder what that shot caller thought. I wondered what he thought while bench pressing three hundred and fifty pounds, when he looked up and saw me holding a hundred pound donut over his face — and drop it!

I wonder what he thought, right about then.

130

DEAR JOHN...

Smokey

You may speak of a movement or sit on a seat,
Have a passage or stool — or simply excrete,
Or say to others "I'm Going out Back"
And groan in pure joy in that smelly old shack.
You can go lay a cable or do number two,
Or sit on the toidy and make a doo doo;
But Ladies and Men who are socially fit,
Under no provocation will go take a shit.

illustration by Daniel Clowes

Seems each generation looks back to an earlier time for reminders of a pleasant past. It's a human trait, I guess, to remember the best and forget the rest. The old days, properly aged, become the good old days. Perhaps that explains my interest in outhouses. In my early years I helped my father build an outhouse behind a cabin on a small lake in northern Minnesota.

Dad was a particular sort and finicky about the design and placement of what he called the "path." He referred to our homemade cabin as a "wilderness home with five rooms and a path." The little house had to match the construction of the cabin, right down to the miniature hip roof and log slabs that laced through each other at the corners, like the intertwining fingers of a man in deep contemplation.

The outhouse had to open to the East, and had to be placed so that the door would not face the cabin. The door had to swing in, which seriously limited the space inside, but Dad had his reasons. The lane from cabin to outhouse was nearly straight, with gentle curves to add class. Trees were planted on either side of the door to create a "fetching entrance."

Inside, we built a multi-sided stool instead of a simple plank seat, and on the stool we placed a genuine toilet seat and lid. A vent connected the stool assembly to the outside through an enclosed chute that led to the roof. A sack of lime took up residence in the corner, with a long-handled dipper hanging nearby ready to neutralize each deposit. Two small screened windows high on opposite walls provided cross-ventilation. The shape of those vents was the topic of family discussion. Moons? Stars? Perhaps an owl cut out to go along with the family name of Weis, pronounced "Wise." I have forgotten just what shape was finally used, since the discussion dwindled when the difficulty of cutting intricate patterns in the log siding became evident.

It's not likely my father ever read the little 18-page booklet written by Chic Sales entitled *The Specialist*. This charming little essay, in bound form, sold over a million copies in dozens of countries. It detailed the thoughts of a man who specialized in building outhouses. He does present some very good ideas, most of which my father incorporated into his masterpiece as a matter of common sense.

For example, the East facing door let one view the sunrise during the morning's constitutional — and that's where the inward-opening door was essential. One could hold the door open with a foot, but quickly shut the door and hold it shut should another customer arrive. It would be awkward with an out-swinging door. A person could find himself exposed while leaning out the door, feeling for the handle.

The straight path was a matter of efficiency, especially for nocturnal use. As Chic put it, "that ain't no time to but stumbling around on some winding path."

An uncle of mine used to brag of tipping ten crappers over one Halloween night. My uncle, and most other folk like to use the term "crapper," but I always considered it a word with a blue tinge, unacceptable in polite conversation. Such is not really the case.

Sir Thomas Crapper was the inventor of a revolutionary valve that permitted a permanently installed bedpot to allow its holdings to be washed down a sewer pipe. His valve involved a trap, or S curve in the bowl, to prevent odors from backing up the pipe, and another valve to shut the flow of flush water, and permit a refill of an overhead tank. But "crapper" had a naughty ring to it, and soon other variations of the word became common. It's one of those rare words that got smutty with use.

When the crapper came into common use, many older homes retrofitted their facilities. Usually an upstairs room was selected, and part of the floor elevated to allow room for the plumbing to be placed under the stool. This was much easier than tearing up the ceiling of the room below. That platform gave rise to the term, "throne," and the room became the "throne room," a noble place to situate a crapper. — *Norm Weis*

"Dag nab it. Spooks been usin' the crapper agin'."

Russ Meyer

(continued from page 47)

But "Beyond" was released as an X.

Yea, which they had no choice. They had no choice and it was early in the game when they had X-rated. They didn't know what to do about it. But at least, I must say, I was able to talk to Dick Zanuck. Yea, straightforwardly. I said, "It's my best picture, and if it's handled right it'll go through the roof. Get a theater on Hollywood Boulevard, let a lot of talk goose it up. And it worked. Zanuck backed me on that. Distribution just wanted to throw it out there. I beat the brain trust. But good.

So success means two years at the majors. If your suitcase was broken, you could send it over to one of the shops that do repair. I had George Stevens' former office suite. It was marvelous. It had a murphy bed you could flip out of the wall. They gave me a Corvette Stingray. I had access to the producers dining room, where you could drink and have steaks prepared for you at night. And [CEO Darryl] Zanuck's personal sauna and swimming pool. It's wonderful! I could have reunions with my army friends. If they want to come over, I said, "Jesus Christ! Let's do it!"

And there was a good place to hide out from my old lady, Edy. She used to get on the warpath. See, I'd bury my car somewhere and tell the guard, "My old lady's coming around looking for me." Also bring a woman around at night occassionally and go ahead and cheat on her. The guards were great. If you were bringing in women, what the hell, nobody needed to know. The cop volunteering, "No, I haven't seen him."

Also, Edy and I would go into Zanuck's private sauna. Yea, we'd get it on there, and she'd always bring this Cold Duck. It's like champagne. I think she wanted me to have a heart attack or something. It would get hotter than hell and she would want to fuck like hell on the floor. I remember one time, the guy who did *Police Story* — What's his name? Hell of a good chap, producer. He went in and stepped right on my back when I was atop of her. He couldn't see because of the steam. And Edy said, "Oh! That's good! Do it again!" [Laughs.] She's all right. I tell you, the gal was OK. She had a beauty. [Indicates picture.] You can see what she looked like. She didn't have the biggest tits in the world, but she had a great body. Every night when we were speaking, we'd have a great time in the rack!

We haven't talked about music in your films. You seem to prefer a jazzy, dramatic score. What sort of music do you like personally?

I like the music of the '30s and '40s, probably orchestras you don't even know. Ambrose. Louie Levy. Who's that guy — Ray Noble. You probably don't know these people. They're great. Great. Standards, you know. Gershwin. Ambrose was one of the leaders of jazz as we know it today. Pieces of music like "Taran-

tula" and "Copenhagen." Real bouncy stuff. He used to backstop Bing Crosby in the later years. So today my favorite music is Ray Coniff, loud as I can play it.

When you're scoring a film, how do you choose the music?

I produce a mixture of country-western and "fortress of God," you know, really heavy Shostakovich or whatever would be available to me. Strauss music. I like a lot of good Nazi music. "Horst Wessel Lied," "Deutschland Uber Alles." And a good kind of what I call '40s jazz. '30s, '40s jazz, the ones we danced to, things like that. I'll use some rock music but it's not my, you know, taste.

What is your taste in wine or liquor? Do you have a favorite drink?

I stopped drinking, then started up again (with care) when my autobiography took over most of my time. I liked Bombay Gin. But now I look forward to one Absolut martini a night.

Yesterday, you mentioned meeting Hemingway in Europe during the war. Are you a fan of his work?

No. Never read one of his books, but I should have.

Really? Not one?

No, I've seen the movie *For Whom the Bell Tolls.* I'm not an avid reader. But I'll read Len Deighton. I like him. He's shot down because the Russians are our friends now. What happened is the poor guy's got a whole new trilogy, *Hook, Line and Sinker,* for his shrinking audience. Are you familiar with Len Deighton?

Yes. Game, Set and Match.

Yea, yea. And then this guy who — I can't remember his name — writes about Detroit. Yea, Elmore Leonard. I love his stuff.

Are you familiar with a cartoonist by the name of Bill Ward? We mention him because we see a certain parallel between his work and yours.

Mr. Ward will have in the neighborhood of sixty-five "bustoons" in my book. I commissioned them, and he drew them to script. And they are largely (in the truest sense) women that I couldn't use a photograph of, although I had some but Edy destroyed a lot of photographs. The tits were bigger than hers. Because the book is so pictoral, I just had him draw up sixty-five cartoons with big, gigantic tits. They're marvelous. Particularly those of Mrs. Buxton, pregnant. I had a slew of pictures of this one woman. But I still wouldn't be able to use her in the volumes because she's married. And has kids. Whereas the publication sports a substantial number of photographs embellished with a paper bag covering her face. Yea, a paper bag. Even on Bill Ward's "bustoons" concerning the same buxotic. Marvelous stuff. It could be a highpoint of the volumes.

Do you have more movies in your head that you'd like to make, that you didn't get the chance to make?

...BOSOM MAXIMUS!
The Munificent "TUNDI"
...setting a NEW Russ Meyer Standard by which all future Bosomania will be measured!

Well, I always had a chance to make them, and I made them for a period of time. I believe I arrived at just the right time. My genre of films were hellishly successful those number of years ago, and now they've been rediscovered via video. I have seventeen titles in release. And the very same genre would work even more today. Why? There's a lot more dirty young men around.

Kitten Natividad

I've even considered that each film could be produced over again. With bigger tits, of course. Consider then, in the case of *Lorna*, the ever-present safety valve. People could sin, do all sorts of unspeakable horrors, but then finally having to pay the piper. If not, you got into trouble with the prosecutors. There weren't any censors. Just prosecutors. The thing to do is show Lorna's flipside. Yea, turn it all around. Sure, the husband's still the cuckold. Hell, Lorna even cheats on the convict. And the bloke doesn't die. He runs off with Lorna's aunt, Tami Roché. She's got great big beautiful tits, *naturellement*. And the husband continuing to remain the cuckold. Why not? Every good Russ Meyer movie deserves a cuckold. This time, no one paying the tab. Including Lorna. No Sodom and Gomorrah for her. No desecration of her heaving/soaring breastworks by a rusty ice tong. Still screwing anybody that moves ... the UPS man, whatever. That's the way I'd do it today. And forget all that bullshit built-in kind of armor just in case you had to be defended. So I think all of the films could be done all over again. Done better. And with bigger girls! Just give some thought to *Supervixens II ... The Bra of God!*

What is Russ Meyer's idea of heaven?

[Looks around himself.] This was heaven. Now it's Palm Desert, CA. Oh, short of being, you know with my mom. Heaven for me would be to be able to spend a week with everybody I've loved and liked. That being man, woman and beast. Just one week. Roll back the time. And then to disappear in a clap of thunder. Yea, my idea of heaven.

How would you like to be remembered?

Ebert should be here. How does he put it? Yea, there was this guy Charles Keating who was on my past case and is very much in the news today. The big swindle. Lincoln Savings. Keating, former head honcho of the Citizens for Decent Literature. The elite of the porn busters. Grandmothers in tennis shoes. And what success he enjoyed. He got to *Vixen*, his primo target ... stopping it cold in the sovereign state of Ohio. I spent a quarter of a million dollars. Tried to put me in jail, but lawyer Elmer Gertz, a tiger of jurisprudence, stood fast in his rabid path. Ebert says it best on RM's epitaph. Keating volunteered something like this: "Russ Meyer has done more to undermine the morals in these United States than anyone else. "And my retort would be: "I was glad to do it."

Readers interested in obtaining Russ Meyer's films on video, or his autobiography, may write to RM Films International, Inc. P.O. Box 3748 Hollywood, CA 90078. Or telephone: (213) 466-7791.

"You can find the damnedest mirages!"

LEETEG

(continued from page 27)

Like Jack Kerouac, another redneck American original, Edgar Leeteg never outgrew his mother. The tragic sense of loneliness and emptiness that haunted him after the age of forty came from the belated realization that this had vitiated his life and estranged him from all other women. As the years passed and Bertha's health declined, he cut his drunken Tuesdays back to fortnights, and compulsively built one addition after another onto the "Villa Velour." Neighbors protested that his building mania was ruining Paopao Bay. In reply to their threats, lawsuits, and ostracism, he scorned and caluminated them, and thumbed his nose with his "Chick Sales." It was the most expensive, luxurious, and altogether resplendent privy in the Southern Hemisphere. The "Aloha Barney," named for the way his dealer signed his letters, was a pink bungalow that took a year to build and remained empty after Davis' single visit in 1952. Three other brightly painted houses in the village, intended for wives that never materialized, attracted an endless procession of freeloaders, barflies, wastrels, sex maniacs, and tourists.

Despite all the distractions, Leeteg managed to produce an estimated 1,694 paintings in fifteen years. He shipped them out in lots, repeating many of his own compositions as well as a few he borrowed from other artists. He took orders for images on demand, sending them off to Barney Davis using a numbering system they developed for the most popular ones to hedge their bet against commercial failures. As the demand for certain images soared, he came to depend on using photographs of these "super dupers" to save set up time and modeling costs. He usually took his own photos, but was also naively under the impression anything found in a magazine was fair game. This accounts for a whole series of portraits of Navajo Indians in an otherwise Polynesian oeuvre, heavy on evocative tropical landscapes and ample breasted Vahinies. When he learned the popular Breck shampoo-esque cameo "Head of Christ" he was filling orders for was copyrighted by Warner Sallman, he stopped production. He wrangled with other artists and photographers whose images he stole, insisting that his thefts were a form of flattery. The testimony of the "Coconut Casanova" to the protean sexual appetite of all great artists was unequivocal:

I lay most of my models ... I've already got a swell l'il sixteen year old native girl lined up for some nudes. That's why I'm sick. I kept her up all night to study her charms and strained myself ... Guess I gotta realize I'm getting old.

On Saturday night, February 7, 1953, the Leeteg legend reached its climax. After a reportedly subdued farewell dinner at Les Tropiques for the crew of the "Philante," he was thrown off the back of a speeding Harley-Davidson as it hit an S curve on the way to the Lido in Papeete. The group was to reconnoiter there for some serious drinking. He died instantly at the age of 49. The angel of Paul Gauguin, whose name had been so handily used to wake the world up to Leeteg of Tahiti, must have been looking down that night on the feisty little maverick. The day before Edgar William Leeteg climbed aboard the motorcycle that killed him, word had already spread as far as Punaavia that he had a sickness the girls should stay away from. He had worked his way through penicillin, streptomycin, and the sulfas. No known drug could cure it.

"Hang on to your hat, Al . . . This is mating season!"

Mrs. Hanson's Secret

(continued from page 37)

her too red and full lips. Mikey whimpered in the back of his throat and couldn't get his lighter to work.

She stood up and came around the bar towards him. She was packed tight tight tight into a piece of clothing that didn't have enough material to be properly called a dress. Her breasts threatened to burst through the top, her waist pulled it in like the pinch of an hourglass, and her hips swelled out to try to bust it out again. Her drop-dead proportions gave a taut little jiggle when she walked because they were stacked on a pair of legs which came out of skyscraper heels and went all the way up to her ass.

Mikey got the lighter to work and set fire to the filter-end of his cigarette, which was when she stood beside him.

He could smell her deadly perfume and feel the sultry heat of her body, she was that close. Mikey's breathing stopped and his heart rate passed the speed of sound. She leaned in to the paralyzed Mikey, a stray lock of blonde hair falling over one of her half-lidded eyes, and said in a voice like smoke,

"I'm drinking scotch," followed by a brief pause, lazy smile, briefer pause, and slow lick of her tongue against those lips, again.

Somehow, Mikey managed to get the cigarette out of his mouth and ordered the pagan goddess a "S-s-s-s-s-sc-sc-scotch..."

Before the drink was served, she whispered hot and moist into his ear, "Come back to my place and I'll give you the best night of sex you ever had."

Instead of having a massive coronary, Mikey managed to nod his willingness. Thank you, God.

Cigar store Indians are more at ease than Mikey was, standing rigidly just inside her bedroom door. His eyes were so wide that he didn't have a forehead left. There was an idiotic, cracked smile on the rest of his face. He couldn't hear for the roar of blood in his ears. Luckily, she wan't saying anything, but she was showing didn't help.

As if it were the second skin of a snake, she peeled off her dress with the devastating grace of a stripper, leaving only bra, panties, stockings and heels. The bra came off next, exposing two mountains of glory that didn't need to rely on a mere bra for support. Then she hooked her thumbs into the elastic of her

panties, threw a look of burn-or-go-blind at Mikey, and slipped them down over her hips to reveal—

A chastity belt?

A chastity belt! Real and locked. Really locked.

Mikey's face collapsed.

She watched and laughed, low and husky. "Oh, it's real, baby. My husband makes me wear it when he's out of town. And he doesn't give me the key." She laughed again.

Mikey's face stayed slack.

"Sorry to tease you," she said with a wicked smile, "but teasing is the only fun I get when I have to wear this."

Suddenly, Mikey smiled. A genuine smile. Not stiff. Not nervous. In control. He didn't stutter when he said, "Hope you meant what you said about the sex," and deftly picked up a bobby pin from her vanity.

Mikey was a locksmith.

He grinned when the lock snapped open.

She grinned when the chastity belt came off. Underneath was something the size of which went with her big tits, wide hips, and long legs: an eight inch cock.

It was still the best night of sex Mikey ever had.

"I just got laid."

YO HO HO . . . AND A BOTTLE OF RUM

(continued from page 52)

sort of drink, as it is today.

In proof thereof, I call as a witness no less a person than Benjamin Franklin, a knowing man, and of more than local repute. He tasted this Rum Punch while traveling to Philadelphia from one of his many excursions, found it so worthy of preservation that he methodically wrote it down, according to the testimony:

    4 ounces of lime juice
    6 ounces of pineapple juice
    10 ounces of orange juice
    1 full quart of light rum
    1 quart of sparkling mineral water

The ingredients were blended, poured over a block of ice from the ice house of the tavern, garnished with wild strawberries and orange slices. This gentleman may not have been the Benjamin Franklin you may recall. I seem to remember that he owned a high-grade bar and grill in Philadelphia, which does not detract from the goodness of this pleasant drink. A scoffer who may have confused the Benjamin Franklins may raise his voice and claim that he doubts if there was sparkling water in the colonial days—he might be set back on his heels if informed that Vichy water was often shipped to these shores as ballast in the sailing ships.

There is a legend, undoubtedly slightly spurious, that the first cocktail in cracked ice was made of rum, milk, sugar, nutmeg and ginger, shaken in a silver pot.

The Punches were numerous; the tavern keeper who could produce one that had real merit was on his way to fame and fortune. Poems, of a sort, in toast form, were drunk, and the words were these:

    One part of "sour" (lime juice)
    Two parts of "sweet" (brown sugar)
    Three parts of "strong" (rum)
    Four parts of "weak" (water and ice)

There is no end to the drinks made of rum in the early history of this country, and not a few of them stemmed from physicians. A Syllabub, for example, "To Prevent Sweating in Ye Bedd from Aches & Paynes," as noted in "The American Drink Book," a fine and handsome volume by S. S. Field, went like this:

> "Into Ye heavy cream put a Good
>   Measure of
> strong Syder (Applejack) and some
>   Sugar
> Whip until it Peeks, stirring in as
>   Much Rumme
> as Ye Cream will Hold. Put fine
>   Nutmeg on Top!"

I find the ancient recipes fascinating and provocative. The proportions are most indefinite, and a liberal-minded individual might go astray, but with the firm and woozy knowledge that he had at least used every ingredient mentioned!

The Beverage Media Blue Book for 1954-55 provides this capsule data on modern rums, and I consider their findings to be reliable:

"Rum's types are identified with their producing regions. Puerto Rico's and Cuba's light rums are dry, delicate, potent with slight molasses flavor and brandy-like taste. Virgin Islands' rums lean to the heavier side, Jamaica's full-bodied rums, like other British West Indies rums, are rich, pungent with bouquet. Demerara's type is heavier-bodied and slightly bolder in taste, although less pungent than Jamaica. Domestic rums are also full-bodied."

Rum almost became our national drink through the whimsey of sheer circumstance. It was cheap, it was available, people liked it so well that the annual consumption was

4 gallons per capita. This happens to be far and away beyond the current consumption of our 1¼ gallons of *all distilled spirits.* A robust people, our ancestors! Even the Puritans thought a little medicinal or ceremonial rum was not impious. Our ancestors regarded rum with deep affection. They were a race of sturdy, catch-as-catch-can tipplers, and, to their credit it must be said that they handled their liquor with a certain amount of decorum.

We still like rum, and our liking is slowly but inevitably going into the upper brackets. Recently, our shipments from Puerto Rico topped the two and a half million gallon mark, and is still rising.

Not all bar men know how to handle rum drinks. The raised eyebrow, the akward fumbling for ingredients, the abashed and embarrassed visage usually betokens the inept bar man. If you know rum drinks, the first taste will confirm your private opinion that the mixer was a lout in spades.

In New Orleans, I find that rum drinks are made deftly and with the skill that comes of long experience. My good friend, Roy Alciatore, the owner of Antoine's Restaurant, the oldest restaurant in these more or less United States under the ownership of the one family—Roy and his cohorts in the spiritual side of his business do a splendid job. If you have the time, slip down to New Orleans, tell Roy you want a Louisiana Lullaby and tell him I sent you. You will have something very special, I assure you, and here's how it is put together.

    1 oz. Puerto Rico rum
    ¼ oz. Dubonnet
    1 dash Grand Marnier
    Squeeze of lemon

Stir with ice, pour into a chilled glass ringed with sugar. It will make a convert of you, if you are a heretic.

Owen Brennan, proprietor of Brennan's Restaurant and the Old Absinthe House, did one he called the Pirate's Dream that was more than middlin' good. A genial host, a fine and loyal friend, his sudden death last year shocked a multitude of sad friends. He made it in this way:

    Juice of 1 orange
    ½ oz. Grenadine
    Juice of 1 lemon
    2 dashes Angostura bitters
    Fresh green mint
    Cherries, 8 to 10 for each drink
    2 oz. each white & gold
        Puerto Rican Rum

Take a huge glass capable of holding 26 to 28 ounces. Crush a few sprigs of green mint into the glass, then add the Rum Grenadine, orange and lemon juice and bitters. Make sure mint is well blended into the ingredients. Fill glass with crushed ice with cherries throughout. Decorate rim with slice of lemon and orange. You'll need plenty of straws for the long pull to the bottom of the glass.

Rum's sort of eternal. Once you have savored its spicy aromatic goodness, you are enthralled forever by its charm and suave sophistication, and you will be beset to know how many ways it can be used—and there are thousands of sure-fire recipes at your finger-tips.

Anyone got a loggerhead?

Scotched

(continued from page 53)

prohibition when demand to produce bootleg whisky caused quality to be sacrificed for quantity and Campbeltown's scotch reputation suffered for it. The city had more than 30 distilleries.

When the crash of 1929 hit, no one would buy the Campbeltown product and the distilleries closed up. Aye, never lower your standards to met fleeting demand. Nowadays Campbeltown is used to describe and style of scotch, although only two distilleris survive, Springbank and Glen Scotia.

The American prohibition whisky-runner, Captain William McCoy's name became the byword for good whisky, "the real McCoy." Aye, to forbid is to give the highest recommendation.

One night after a wee dram of Laphroaig with salty sea breeze elegance and a peat-smoke taste, I did visit Angus Podgorney. Laphroaig being one of the only distilleries left that proudly floor-malts their barley to guarantee the peat-reek. After splitting a tappit hen (equal to three English pints) of Bunnahabhain, a most delicate Islay single malt, I bid snoring Angus good evening and rested under a tree. I slept instantly, the throat awash with the Islay magic and my body was aglowing in the robust sea air. A couple of lascivious lassies found my slumbering body and did proceed to handle my bagpipe upon which they took turns composing lovely tunes.

George Smith, a Highlander by descent, seeing that the future was to be with legitimate distilling, was the first to take out a license. The illicit distilleries did not take this act lightly and threatened George. Nothing ever came of the threats. King George IV drank only the Glenlivet and nothing else. By decree only George Smith could produce "The Glenlivet." All the

other 25 distilleries would have to be using Glenlivet with a hyphen after their own name, such as Dufftown-Glenlivet and Glenkeith-Glenlivet.

I've journeyed to Glasglow once, when the Auchentoshan distillery in the Kilpatrick Hills on the river Clyde was needing a stillman. Auchentoshan is a Lowlands malt that is distilled three times, while most other scotches are distilled twice. As a result, Auchentoshan has the delicate and milder taste that is commonly associated with the Lowland-style scotches. The Lowlands produce gentle, lighter and sweeter whisky as opposed to the Highlands' wild, lusty and peaty flavors. The only other thrice-distilled scotch is another Lowlands whisky, Rosebank with a light sherry sweetness.

On my return to the northern parts during my twenty-second summer, I was met by an auburn-haired bar maid in Aberdeen. The Glen Garioch distillery was closed for the summer months owing to the heat, and the men of Oldmeldrum were needed in the quarry. She took me round the granite buildings at mid-day with fiddle, bread, cheese and whisky. We stomped and fiddled until sweat was whipped into a lather. Now, I wouldn't be recommending that Glen Garioch be lapped up from the well of a lassies cleavage, but you wouldn't miss the smooth, long throat of taste.

My love of single malt scotch can be explained by a story Aunt Mary used to tell. One day a woman with a child in her arms and another bit thing at her knew met among them during field work. The horn cup was handed to her and she took a "gey guid drap" herself and then gave a little to each of the babies. "My goodness child," Said Aunt Mary to the wee thing that was trotting by the mother's side, "doesn't it bit you?" "Aye, but I like the bite." replied the creature.

TRUMPET AND SPIKE

(continued from page 69)

and be handed over with a smile, for a small sum of money, a box of Palfium tablets. I began to breathe a little more freely for the first time in years. But once again I felt that this would be easier if I changed my surroundings. Paris was getting like Harlem — full of junkies from way back home. One day I packed my bag and went off to Italy — Milan to be precise — where I had a few friends, leaving Helema in Pais, with Henry, our boy. Things didn't work out as I expected them to.

Instead of cutting down on Palfium, I was perpetually increasing the doses. As a result I began to suffer dreadful hallucinations. I wired Helema in Paris four words: "Come, I need you." Helema, with me, never knew anything but fear, worry, misery and poverty, and was even arrested once and accused of aiding and abetting me. She now came to Milan where we took a small apartment and I tried to kick the stuff.

Then a terrible thing happened. It seemed that doctors had discovered at last what I could have told them in the first place, that Palfium was really habit-forming drug. One fine morning I read in the papers that the governments of France, Italy and Belgium had placed the stuff on the Register of Dangerous Drugs. Overnight it became impossible to buy the junk without a doctor's prescription. A real nightmare hunt for prescriptions for Palfium began for me. A doctor would give me a prescription for a box of tablets — that is for four tablets, which is the quantity in one box. But I was taking 24 tablets a day, dissolved into about 30 injections! So you see why I had to visit six doctors each day for six prescriptions.

Life became real hell. My horn was my one consolation and my hope. Without it I think I would have died. And do you know, I never played so well — like Charlie Parker when he was dying. People told me so and I knew it. There was a jam session in Liege, Belgium, and I drove there as a dodge. Once in Liege, I drove like a madman across the Belgian frontier into Germany where Palfium was still

off the Dangerous Drug List and could be bought openly and I brought back an enormous amount. I pulled up at a gasoline station back in Lucca, Italy and went into the washroom and gave myself a huge dose of Palfium. It was an overdose, like the one Dick Twardzick had given to himself, and I just managed to get back to the car before passing out. Anyway they rushed me off to the hospital in an ambulance and once there they kept me in. When I came out of the hospital I was taken straight to the calaboose and locked up. They tried me and gave me a year, of which I did eight months in Lucca's prison. Since then I've been in other jails in Europe and I can assure you that after them, American prisons are de luxe hotels. Lucca, I think, is one of the worst jails in Europe. It was a dungeon, man. I spent the whole winter there — lying in a sort of stupor, shivering and moaning and talking to myself, while the rats and the beetles and the lice and the fleas crawled at leisure all around me.

At the beginning of my stay in Italy I met Carol, who was in show business like myself. She's British, from London. She came out to Milan with a variety show. I think it was love at first sight with us, though it was some weeks before we confessed as much to each other. And I confessed much more to her — all about my life as a junkie and the hell that it was. "Chet," she said, "you'll have to give that up or you'll kill yourself and I don't want you to die."

She followed me all around Italy — to Bologna, Florence, Rome, wherever I went. She stuck to me in spite of everything. When I was in a nursing home she would visit me every day; she was in court when I was put on trial, and she helped and encouraged me when I was locked up. They let me out after eight months, as I told you, then Carol and I split to Germany as fast as we could.

Palfium, you will recall, was still sold freely there. But a terrible disappointment was in store for me. While I'd been in the jug, Germany had joined Italy and France and put Palfi-

um on the Dangerous Drug List. I had no connections in Germany, and if I wanted my daily doses of Palfium this meant a wild race around Munich. Instead, I stole a bunch of blank prescriptions from a doctor's office. I went straight back to my hotel and filled them in. Not knowing German I had to tell the druggist a cock-and-bull story about my being American and that for this reason the doctor had made out the prescription in English. It could never have worekd. The proof is that the druggist after asking me politely to wait a moment, went off into the back of his shop and telephoned the police. When I saw the Black Maria in front of the door I knew I was lost. I had become a thief as well as a junkie. This was headlined in the press, as might have been expected. I was kept in a Munich jail for a couple of months and then I was bound over and expelled from the Federal Republic.

It so happened that Scott Brown, the drummer, was run in in Munich the same time I was for having junk on him. We were expelled together. We were barred from entering Germany for three years and taken under police escort to the Swiss frontier. I went into a Zurich nursing home and when I came out I decided to go to England. Carol was expecting a baby and naturally she wanted to have it at home. In my own case, I thought it would be a good idea to start all over again in a new country. I was off junk and I wanted to go steady and I was certain I would be signed for different engagements in London. But in order to get a job I needed a permit from the Ministry of Labour. If it hadn't been for Carol being English and expecting the baby I would have told them to stick their country. But I won't criticize the English about the way they handle drug addicts. They're the only civilized country in the world in this respect. You can register as a drug addict and obtain a doctor's prescription, free of charge under National Health Service and walk into any druggist and buy your dose of junk.

Things began to look up in spite of my not having a permit to work. I managed to do the music with an English orchestra for the film *Sum-*

mertime. Unfortunately, the junk was to ruin all my plans in England. You can get your fix openly in Britain, but junkies from all over the world would be running there if you could get any amount you wanted. The fix is a small one, given to you with the hope that you'll be able to kick the stuff. And to me it was soon useless. I needed more — much more. I managed to obtain a fair supply on the black market until one day a bastard druggist squealed about me to the cops and I was quickly run into Brixton jail.

While I was locked away, Carol gave birth to our son Dean. I was worrying about where to go next. Because I was eventually convicted as a drug addict, bound over and ordered to leave the country. That's why I decided to go right back home to the United States. But here again was a hitch. When Helema had left for home I had sent her the money to divorce me. But it now appeared that she hadn't done so. Once again I don't blame her. I was always short of money and she was getting mighty little from me. No wonder she had used that divorce money for housekeeping. But this meant that my marriage to Carol was not valid and that my son Dean was illegitimate. Consequently, no visa could be issued for Carol and Dean and that meant, as far as I was concerned, goodbye to Uncle Sam. I arrived at Dover with Carol and Dean and a police escort and sailed to France. We had little money and took a small place in Montmartre at first, and I can't say finding a job was easy. In the end I was engaged to play in a small nightclub on the Left Bank — The Fishing Cat — and I'm glad to say that I soon became a star turn.

When I left England for France, I knew something had changed. I could feel it in my bones, but I refused to believe it, I was so terrified of getting hooked again. A change had come over me — don't ask me how, don't ask me why. Months had gone by since I'd taken hard stuff and I hadn't the slightest desire to start off again. I've never played better. When I played some of my old successes like "Bye-Bye Blackbird" and "Summertime" I brought the house down. For the first time since I started ten years

before, I felt no need for junk. I can say to myself, "Chet, you did it once for six months, you can do it again." I'll tell you something that should really convince you. A few weeks ago when Ray Charles was in Paris with his band, the French police ran in David "Fathead" Newman, Kenny Drew and Larry Ritchie, and all were accused of dope trafficking. As I'm maybe the best known junkie or should I say, ex-junkie, among all the cats in Europe, the coppers came rushing up the stairs and hammering on my door. They figured they might as well rope me in with the others. They made me undergo a very severe medical examination. In the end they certified me to be completely cured. Understand me, man, there were sad faces among the cops.

Yes, Dear

(continued from page 73)

good job of it, Charles told himself. Agnes never liked anything half done. He lifted the statue again and brought the bloody base down on her head twice more. Agnes collapsed and lay still.

Charles stood looking down at her for a moment an then he went into the bathroom and washed his hands. Then he wiped off the statue of the dog and returned it to the shelf. He looked again at the body on the floor and shook his head. An ugly stain was spreading over the polished floor.

"Agnes wouldn't like that, she wouldn't want the floor messed up that way." He laughed and was startled at the sound for he hadn't laughed in years. He caught the body under his arms and dragged it toward the cellar door. It was fortunate that Agnes had him cementing in the coal bin in his spare time. It would be easy to cement her in there. It was also fortunate that Agnes had told everyone that she was going to her mother's. He'd have a week, maybe longer, before anyone missed her and then just let them try to find her.

After he finished in the cellar, he returned to the living room and mopped up the floor before fixing him-

self a light supper. Afterwards he took down his stamp album and worked on it for a couple of hours before going to bed.

He was almost dressed the next morning, when it started. He checked to see if his tie was on straight and before he could stop himself, he said, "Yes, dear."

Somewhere within him, the voice began. "Do you have a clean handkerchief?"

"Yes, dear."

"Do you have the ticket? You have to take it back and get the money."

"Yes, dear." He managed to suppress a scream. Agnes was dead but her domination was so strong that she was still with him.

"You'd better hurry, Charles." He grabbed his hat and almost ran out the door. He had to get away. He had to get away from Agnes.

"You'll be late if you don't hurry."

"Yes, dear." He let his hands drop from him face and started to put them in his pockets.

"Don't put your hands in your pockets, Charles."

"Yes, dear ... I mean no, dear."

"Why are you loitering, Charles?"

He started to walk slowly down the walk. "Hurry, Charles, hurry!"

"Yes, dear."

"Why are you walking so slowly? Are you ogling those women, Charles?"

"No, dear."

He was at the station now and the 8:35 was just looming up, a half-minute away from the station. Its brakes began to squeal and in a moment its wheels would be grinding to a stop.

"Charles," the voice in his mind said. Charles knew what the last question was. "Charles, are you zipped up?"

"Charles, are you zipped up?" the voice came again, but Charles Henry didn't answer. At that moment, the train had neatly zipped off the head that he had thankfully laid in its path.

Fine Art of Training Strippers

(continued from page 115)

stage, just as every one in a man's can be used in the ring. My Cherokee chick now has complete control of every muscle in her delectable body. Gaining this control took a lot of work but it has paid off in top billings and large salaries that are among the top ten in stripperdom.

Training is not only important to gaining skill, but to maintaining looks. Lots of the girls who doff their clothes for money depend on their after-show drinking ability instead of their talent for their salaries. They work in upholstered sewers where two years of constant drinking can wash them up. I have seen a lot of young girls start in the business, and two years later they look 15 years older that they are. A girl in the stripping line has to watch her health and stick to a rigid conditioning routine to keep the body that men — and women — admire.

In this, strippers are just like fighters, who must stay at a fine edge of conditioning as long as they are going to win in the ring.

In building Do-May's acts, we strive to emphasize this beautiful black-haired, blue-eyed chick's Indian background. She is half Cherokee and half Irish, and that is a high-voltage combination, believe me.

In her numbers, which are always set in Indian motifs, with ample use of fringed buckskin, eagle feathers and similar props, we recapture the fire and passion of the traditional Indian dances, using a totem pole as a central prop to provide focus for her movements.

I like the way Do-May described her number to a newspaper reporter who pressed her for more detailed description of what she does on stage.

"Well," she replied, busily tying her moccasin strings, "my Indian dance is quite different from most. You might say that I make love to the totem pole."

Even this is something of an understatement, and another writer who saw the show said, "It was doubtful which were more goggle-eyed, the four little men on the totem-pole or the numerous optics of the spectators."

One interesting thing that I have learned is that it is not sufficient to merely satisfy the men in an audience for a girl to be a success. She must also be appreciated by the women. When a stripper can get women to come and see her as well as men, then she is on the way to being a top drawing name. Theaters and cabarets couldn't suvive on male patronage alone, and the women are the ones who make the difference between profit and loss in many cases.

Women seem to like the color and fire of Do-May's act as wll as men, and often are far more appreciative of the careful selection of costumes, music and action that the men are. Dorothy Kilgallen, the famous columnist, expressed their reactions in her comment that "Do-May's Indian costumes are just too colorful and beautiful to describe, her dancing superb, and her musical arrangements are so authentic that you can expect to see a tribe of redskins to ride by at any time." When I read that, I knew we had succeeded with Do-May.

Women are also especially fascinated by Do-May's control of her pectoral muscles, which gives such bounce to her bosom. They watch avidly as she displays her skill on stage, then often come back and ask her how she does it. She explains that it takes great patience and lots of practice, and can't be done overnight. Just the same, nine out of 10 of these curious maids and matrons go home and try it, then come back and tell her about it the next night.

On one occasion, a really pretty gal came back three or four times for further instruction. Do-May and I were both puzzled, and after a couple of repeats Do-May quizzed her about why she was so interested. The woman confided that she feared her husband was beginning to "look around" and she was desperate for something new to fascinate him.

The happy ending to the story came after we'd moved on to another city, and a wire arrived which announced: "New act big hit. Constant demand for encores. Going on road for second honeymoon next week." You can never tell.

While all of the work is going on in training and polishing the girl, I find that I am also engaged in another side of the business which is very similar to building up a fighter. To make a boy a top money-maker, you must choose his matches carefully, see that he gets the right publicity, and that his name becomes known in the right way.

It's the same way with a stripper. I actually spend about 12 hours a day getting out publicity, building new props, dreaming up gimmicks, doing research for authenticity in production numbers, working with arrangers, and carefully choosing this girl's engagements, in addition to supervising her daily workout routines.

In billing Do-May as the "Cherokee Half-Breed" I followed one of the rules I learned in the fight game — a smart, catchy and easily remembered name with just enough of the unusual to it so that it draws attention.

As a girl rises in the public eye, I become more and more watchful of her. O course, I keep a close check on her figure, and diet. We agree on a set of rules just like training rules for a fighter. When I see a gal gaining weight, I just tell her. "Remember, honey, nobody wants to see a fat gal take her clothes off." That settles them down real fast.

Also, a girl in this business has to watch her personal habits because there are many people waiting to condemn her because she is a strip. The first false step she takes, she gets bad publicity. I don't allow any of my girls to do any excessive drinking, or to be too wild in their private lives.

This really isn't too hard, though, because strippers are good-natured good-hearted gals, who are always willing to lend a helping hand. I will never forget an occasion recently when we were playing St. Louis, and Do-May woke me up early Easter morning.

"Come on, get up," she said.

I opened one bleary eye, wondering what in the world was wrong. After a hard Saturday night's work, every minute of sleep on Sunday is like a gold nugget to a stripper.

"What's up?" I yawned.

"We're going to make a bunch of kids happy," she said. "Come on."

Well, I hauled myself out of the sack and sure enough, Do-May had her Cadillac all filled with boxes of Easter eggs, chocolate bunnies, candy, toy rabbits and all sorts of Easter stuff. And do you know what we did that day? We went out to the Masonic Home in St. Louis and gave it all away to the orphans there. I may be a softie, but it brought tears to my eyes to see this gal, so often condemned by prudes, so happy making alll those little children happy.

Yet there are always those who are eager to jump on strippers at the slightest excuse for being loose-moraled. And it gave me great pleasure one night to see just how such a paragon of virtue made out herself. The gal was overheard remarking: "A girl who could get up there and take her clothes off must really be a tramp." We all bristled, but later we laughed because this guardian of public morals was herself picked up by the police who found her and a gentleman friend in a compromising position in an auto in the parking lot that same night.

I guess it's all in the way you look at things, whether someone is good or bad. There are some people who wouldn't think that counted at all. But I do.

A stripteaser properly trained and built up is a big investment, and a considerable enterprise in herself. Do-May, for example, travels with her personal manager, photographer, costumer, music arranger, publicity agent and a huge van of props. To pro-

tect this investment, I not only school the girls in my stable in the art of disrobing, but also the art of self-defense. It has come in handy for them more times than once, believe me. they can throw a left hook as fast and effectively as they can throw a bump or grind, although to look at them you'd never know they packed such a wallop.

Do-May proved the importance of this training on one occasion in St. Louis. I don't want to give the town a bad name. It's really a swell place to play, but this did happen there. She was on her way to her car after work early one morning, when a man called her by name, "Princess." She turned, and the guy had a gun.

"Gimme your purse," said they thug. Well, this was the last night of the week, and pay day. Do-May was not about to surrender her sizeable roll. So she gave him her purse, right over the head, then knocked the gun out of his hand, and grabbed it. The guy ran, needless to say, and I determined never to let a girl of mine go to work without some self-protection training. Of course, I would be a lot prouder if she'd laid him low with a left hook, but then that's a woman for you. What she did was probably safer in the long run.

I now have six gals under my tutelage, and I'm always looking for more talent. I must admit, that after years with fighters, it's quite a change.

It's a far cry from the old days at the gym, this walking into Do-May's dressing room, all perfumed with cologne and flowers, and having the pulsating experience of watching the gorgeous doll slip into a pair of black mesh hose. What a sight. And it's my job.

Nuts to You

(continued from page 124)

slaughtered, injecting the animals' sex glands into the Pope's sickly tissues. The demonic sacrifice was accorded a success, the Pope's health improving measurably. Among Niehans' more celebritous patients were Gloria Swanson, Somerset Maugham, Noel Coward and the Duke and Duchess of Windsor.

Niehansian therapy exists today in the resort towns of Vevey and Gstaad, Switzerland. The very rich flock to the clinics twice yearly for their rejuvenation shots, composed these days of liquefied sheep fetuses aborted and flash-frozen in Germany for export to Swiss cell therapy clinics. Genesis West is the name of a clinic located in Tijuana which today administers live cell therapy to all those who can afford the near to four thousand dollar price tag. The Swiss clinics, where billionaire Adnan Kashoggi was captured for extradition to the United States for the Imelda Marcos trial, cost quite a bit more.

Meanwhile, might we not take up Voronoff's suggestion to avail ourselves of the vast storehouse of reusable body parts available from those who have met with car crashes or other fatal accidents of fortune? Sex glands can survive six to eight hours beyond their owner's death. For, as Voronoff reports in *The Conquest of Life*: "When the guillotine cuts off the head of a criminal, this head, severed from the trunk, remains alive for some minutes; the brain does not deteriorate instantly; and this head thinks ... If they are removed in time ... organs retain all their vital properties and, if transplanted in another body they are capable of again accomplishing their former functions."

143

FETISHES!

(continued from page 97)

are acts which holy and venerated women have performed." The equation of frustrated sexuality equaling religiosity was quite thoroughly explored by Freud and Wilhelm Reich in the post World War II classic, *The Mass Psychology of Fascism*. Millions of orgastically insufficient women go to church daily to cry their lungs out at the image of the crucifixion, which Freud believed represents the castrated or impotent male. Sexually satisfied women who harbor no guilt for quenching sexual thirst usually derive no catharsis from such religious symbolism. Thus the high percentage of old maids and frigid, secret men-haters at mock orgasmic church ceremonies. Keep out a wary eye for the pious.

• Case No. 11: Krafft-Ebing reports the following interesting subject: "A monk, of a gloomy temperament, was known to be a sleepwalker. One night while his prior sat at the writing desk, absorbed in though, the sleepwalking monk glided into the room, with his eyes wide open, clutching a knife in his hand. He noticed neither the prior seated at the table nor the burning candle; stepping slowly up to the cot he stuck his knife three times into the bedclothes and then walked back to his cell, satisfied. Next morning he confessed to the astonished prior that he had dreamed the prior had killed his mother and that her blood-stained shadow appeared to him demanding revenge. Shortly thereafter, he woke up, found himself lying in his cot, bathed in perspiration, and thanked God that it was only a horrible dream. The monk was astounded when the prior told him what had happened." [Stekel, *Peculiarities of Behavior*, pp. 35-36.]

The acme of sick fuckery comes, of course, with the bizarreries of necrosadistic impulses. Often they lurk under the cover of normalcy:

• "Case No. 31: A 53-year-old, very elegant man is known among [a prostitute's] associates as the sofa stabber. He goes only to those prostitutes who know his mania and are not afraid of him. He undresses himself, murmurs all sorts of wild but completely unintelligible words, throws himself upon the sofa, and stabs it through ever so many times with a knife. Then brief coitus takes place, after which he lies for some time as if unconscious...." [Stekel, *Sadism and Masochism*, Volume II, p. 75.]

• "Case No. 30: Mr. K. H. always has a fowl with him when he goes to a brothel. This fowl he has to strangle before the eyes of the prostitute; then he throws himself upon her and performs coitus with a great orgasm. Without the bird he is completely impotent...." [Stekel, *Sadism and Masochism*, Volume II, p. 74.]

The Whip, The Rod ...

(continued from page 93)

heavy nylon cord to avoid chafing is good and works well with pulley devices if not just simply bound to the headboard (brass bed owners, take note!) or tied up from the legs of the bed. Usually, she may be inclined to only wrap them tightly about her wrists, unknotted, but there are many who prefer the inescapable slipknot.

She should be topless, of course, her back to the mattress. In a carefully phrased explanation you whisper to her that these bonds were newly installed and that you wish her to "try them out." Tremulously, she agrees and, her arms gently pulling at shoulder length, strain gradually at your "urging." With any luck, she may work up a regular sweat and a low light passing over this view beggars description.

Lady Bullfighter

(continued from page 99)

had called me matadora at the San Luis airport when we met, and who I now learned was one of the matadors who were to fight in Juarez on the eighteenth. I still hoped for a chance to make him use the term without the slighest trace of the sarcasm which I had at least imagined had been in his tone; and I was irked that he had a place I'd wanted in the Juarez corrida. Of course he was a full matador and I was silly, since it was not his fault that he had been billed where I wanted to be. He probably didn't know that I had anything to do with it. Alejandro, my teacher, says that jealousy is necessary in the ring, and I guess I felt it then, outside of the ring. At least I was envious. At the same time I was attracted to Montani. He looked like a strong character, had a nice, sensitive mouth, and was most courteous.

When it came to the testing, Montani took the most difficult cows, politely letting me have the best, but even so I was sluggish and the cows were too smart.

"Why don't you make veronicas like Montani?" Alejandro kept yelling.

When he called, "Tiene miedo (have you fear)?" it was the last straw.

"Yes, I'm afraid. So what?" I yelled back. I looked up and Montani was smiling at Don Pepe and Don Ramiro. Again, I remembered the "matadora" at the airport. I wasn't afraid; I was angry at myself and felt ridiculous and humiliated. I'd show them something — that I can fight well, and am serious. I gave Montani a determined glance as I exchanged my cape for the sword and muleta. I wasn't pretty — I was sweaty, disheveled and dirty, but I was going to fight that cow properly, come hell or high water. She was the last of the day, a treacherous cow who learned very quickly.

I measured my steps towards her. I didn't care how temperamental or smart she was. I planted my feet uncompromisingly and offered fight.

She must have understood my determination, for she took the cape and did what I wanted her to do. I had to fight her very close to make her do it, even crossing her to make her think a charge worth her while. She took two high passes, and I went across her to make her charge on the right. She took two beautifully and by the third, she knew — but she didn't let me know she knew. She charged for the muleta and just as she reached it, turned and hooked me inside of the right thigh. It felt like a bee sting as I was lifted up and tossed to the ground. As she stomped on me, I put my arm over my head, waiting for her to quit or be taken off so I could get up and finish her.

Montani caped her away from me. I got up and found my muleta and sword, feeling a little dizzy. Then I felt a draft and looked down to see if I was decent. My pants leg was ripped all the way down to the ankle. Then I saw the hole in my flesh and asked for a handkerchief, impatient to get back to that cow.

"No, no, you're not going back," Alejandro said.

I gave him a look of scorn and started for the cow. I wasn't going to let a puncture keep me from finishing.

"But hombre, you have a cornada (horn wound)," Alejandro said, looking worried.

Most sympathetically, Montani offered to carry me out.

"I can walk," I said, waving him away. Then I noticed how serious everyone looked. They took me into a room and put me on a bed. I thought, perhaps Manolete slept here. Don Pepe's wife came in and they looked at the leg. I didn't want to look at it. I just kept thinking, so this is a goring.

I hadn't realized yet that Montani was probing around, trying to find out how far in the horn had gone and how many trajectories there were. He suddenly touched something that really hurt. I know he had to cut off the pants leg and that he said something about my not minding, since I wouldn't want to wear them again anyway as they were not only torn but soaked with blood.

"Patricia," Don Pepe said, "you know the life of a bullfighter is cornadas y dinero (gorings and money)."

I smiled politely. I really think I was proud that I'd been gored.

145

BEATing Off with Doc Kinsey

(continued from page 71)

So he told Herbert, "I'll tell you what, Mr. Huncke. You can help me greatly if you'd introduce me to some of your friends, so I can interview them as well. In fact, I'll give you two dollars for every subject you can bring me."

Herbert jumped at the chance. "I think I can help you, Dr. Kinsey. Why don't you come back to the Square some evening and I'll introduce you to some good people I know."

When Kinsey first met William Burroughs, the two immediately hit it off. "They spoke the same language," Huncke recalls. "Burroughs became a junkie primarily for scientific reasons. He was well-schooled and very curious." Burroughs and Kinsey — and on occasion, Allen Ginsberg, Jack Kerouac and his wife, Edie Parker, Burroughs' wife Joan Adams, among others — would get together at one of several popular buckets-of-blood around the Square. Such dives as Gilroy's and The Angler. The good doctor Kinsey would remind his new friends of his study, and the Beats, having put on a glow, allowed that they were happy to "compile data."

"Oh, Kinsey was a hit," Huncke remembers. "And he was just delighted with the language! I don't think he'd heard much in the way of so-called street talk before. You know, out front and direct."

It occured to me, as I sat with Huncke, how very intriguing it is that both Dr. Kinsey — pioneering sex researcher largely responsible for a new openness in the discussion of sex both in social and academic communities — and the nascent Beats, writers and personalities who unleashed the spirit of the subterranean world on to the general public, crossed paths on the streets of Times Square.

I asked Huncke, how many people did you end up sending to Kinsey?

"Man! She's way out!"

"I sent a few over, you know that. Yes, sure. I'd get them some bread from Kinsey sometimes. Or else get them a cut of mine," he grins. There's more going on than Huncke lets slip. He hasn't survived these last 75 years without a sense of knowing what to say and knowing when to keep it zipped. Maybe, I point out, some of you more aware cats deliberately fucked up the statistics by exaggerating? You know, wild sex tales of urban yeggs? Wasn't it obvious, correct me now if I'm mistaken, that he wanted this kind of funky dope for the study?

"Well, he was a strange cat, all told," Huncke allows. "I'm sure he had a few pet ideas he explored more thoroughly than the general information. But the man was pure-D science. He did keep coming back for more. He returned for a second visit to New York and this time had a couple of assistants in tow. I guess he must've been getting something he needed."

It's interesting to speculate whether Kinsey's "facts," such as his famous postulation that one out of every three American males experienced a homosexual encounter, are weighted by the contacts Herbert Huncke provided him, the street hustlers, the excitable weekend queens confessing their transgressions.

What couldn't the Beats provide Dr. Kinsey? Huncke admits he couldn't get himself to come off in the doctor's presence. Kinsey requested that Herbert outline his endowment on a phallic-shaped card for measuring purposes, but Huncke says he neglected to go through with that bit of data. "I just did not feel like it. I had to draw the line somewhere."

Can you imagine Ginsberg, expounding and pontificating (having recently met his bisexual lover, Neal Cassady, the renowned cocksman) on the subject of the perfect orgasm, both physical and spiritual? Recall, Ginsberg had his profound vision of Blake after he'd masturbated. Kerouac, being something of a prude, may have avoided an interview with the Kinsey Institute. According to Huncke, his marriage to Edie Parker fizzled because he lacked the resolve in bed — he got off on the typewriter. Conversely, Neal Cassady, *On The Road's* protagonist, is said to have procured sex — with others or by his lonesome — eight times a day.

Perhaps inspired by his meetings with Kinsey, William Burroughs began to formulate his nakedly honest portrayals of men engaged beyond their control in sexual acts bizarre and familiar. Was he at last able, under the spell of the sex doctor, to confirm in his mind the intractable concepts of sexual and junk addiction?

Before the advent of Kinsey's book, much had been learned about human sexuality. It was Dr. Kinsey's contribution to the field of sexuality to provide a statistical foundation; a statistical foundation based in no small part on the proclivities of the swinging Beats. 🎩

Cadwallader
J. Cadd

I Cried, You Didn't Listen
A Survivor's Exposé of the California Youth Authority

by Dwight Edgar Abbott, with Jack Carter

"The most powerful tale of horror within the walls of penal institutions since *Papillon*. The terrifying aspect is that it describes America's juvenile institutions." – Alden Mills, *Arete*. "The author's well-written story comes at the reader fast and furiously, Abbott easily achieving his desired goal of shocking readers into an awareness of the inhumanity of America's juvenile penal institutions." —*Publishers Weekly*. Co-author Jack Carter's afterword investigates the gladiator schools that once held Abbott. Winner, Project Censored Award.

ISBN: 0-922915-08-4 $10.95

The Magician's Dictionary
An Apocalyptic Cyclopædia of Advanced Magic(k)al Arts and Alternate Meanings

by E. E. Rehmus

This eclectic and idiosyncratic volume fills an enormous void in occult research and reference. At last, here's a trenchant and useful guide to *contemporary* occultism and mysticism, navigating through the works of John Whiteside Parsons, Aleister Crowley, Philip K. Dick, Terence McKenna, Kenneth Grant and Robert Wilson, among many others. "Surprising and delightful. I am learning from the book, something I have not said of anything since *Cosmic Trigger* and *Valis*." — Fr. Belarion, *Abrasax*.

ISBN: 0-922915-01-6 $12.95

Tortures and Torments of the Christian Martyrs

by Rev. Antonio Gallonio

The notorious martyrology of Gallonio is augmented in this special Feral House edition with many remarkable illustrations by today's most outré artists (such as S. Clay Wilson, Daniel Clowes, Peter Bagge, Savage Pencil, Sarita Vendetta, many others) and lethal criminals, including Manson, Ramirez, Gacy. Complete with color frontispiece by Joe Coleman and a forensic examination on the death of Christ by pathologists at the Mayo Clinic. Limited quantities available. No longer available in stores.

ISBN: 0-922915-02-4 $25.00

The Manson File

The only book on the marketplace to present the philosophy, language and images of Manson and his family from the inside without the obfuscation of moralistic tongue-cluckings and ulterior motives by the publicity hungry and probation-starved. Feral House has obtained the last remaining stock and is offering them for sale by direct mail only.

$15.00

To Order Feral House Titles:
Send check or money order for cost of book plus $1.75 for first title, $1.25 each additional title, to Feral House, PO Box 861893, Los Angeles, CA, 90086-1893. We do not accept credit card orders. Canadian orders, add $3.00 for first title, $2.50 each additional title. Orders shipped to all other countries, add $4.00 for first title, $3.50 each additional title for surface mail; or $10.00 additionally for each title for air mail service. All non-domestic orders must include check or international money order for US funds drawn on a US bank.

Bookstores: Feral House is distributed to the trade through Publishers Group West (800) 788-3123. Many of our titles are also available from Ingram, Baker and Taylor, Inland, Bookpeople and other regional wholesalers. We are distributed to the trade in England and Europe through Turnaround Distribution, London. Canadian booksellers can obtain Feral House titles through Marginal Distribution or The Book Centre.